A Dog

The Way Some
of Our Closest Friends View Us

A Fireside Book
Published by Simon & Schuster
NEW YORK · LONDON · TORONTO · SYDNEY · TOKYO · SINGAPORE

Roger A. Caras

Is Listening

FIRESIDE

Rockefeller Center
1230 Avenue of the Americas
New York, New York 10020

First Fireside edition, 1993

FIRESIDE and colophon are registered trademarks
of Simon & Schuster Inc.

Designed by Edith Fowler
Manufactured in the United States of America

10 9 8 7 6 5 4 3 2 1
10 9 8 7 6 5 4 3   Pbk.

Library of Congress Cataloging in Publication Data
Caras, Roger A.
    A dog is listening : the way some of our closest
friends view us / Roger A. Caras.
        p.   cm.
    Includes index.
    1. Dogs.   2. Dogs—Behavior.   3. Dogs—
Anecdotes.   4. Senses and sensation.   I. Title.
SF426.C337   1992
636.7'08928—dc20   91-40649
                                                CIP

ISBN: 0-671-70249-1
ISBN: 0-671-79726-3 Pbk.

For
SARAH,
JOSHUA,
ABAIGEAL,
and HANNAH,
a new generation of dog lovers

And for
JILL of Thistle Hill Farm

Frst thoughts, random and otherwise

If you have spent your life with animals as I have (in my case over fifty dogs and at least as many cats), you have inevitably been exposed to a great many animal lovers as well. The two go together and in time it becomes almost impossible to determine what you have learned from one lot and what you have gained by being exposed to the other. The two sources of wisdom blend, which is not taking anything away from either one—it is just the way it is. It would be a much better world I suspect if we didn't try to draw a distinct line between ourselves and the "lower animals," whatever they are, a distinction made in hell that serves no good purpose, just a whole bunch of bad ones. Besides, it never is as clear a demarcation as some of us would like to think. The line is ego-generated and for centuries man has created the science to justify it, but we are undoing much of that now. When paleontologist Louis Leakey reviewed the findings of Jane Goodall who was studying the wild chimpanzees of Gombe, he declared it was time to redefine man. I don't think that has been done very well yet. But while we are in that mode it might serve a real purpose if we tried to redefine the dog as well, and then, perhaps, man and dog as a cohesive social unit.

Toward this end, I am personally grateful both to the animals and the animal enthusiasts I have had the great pleasure of knowing and working with because I have benefited from them in more ways than perhaps even I know.

I have been married to a wholly uncontrollable animal lover for thirty-seven years as of this writing. More people than I can remember have pitied "poor Jill" because she is married to that "animal nut"—meaning me, of course. What they have not realized is that *I* am the sane one. The reason we have, at the moment, only four horses, TJ, Chrissie, Sheba and Sherry, two cows, Steakums and Fat Susan Jane (distinctly pets, not meat reserves), twelve dogs and ten cats, is that I have put my foot down and demanded that we at least try to be *sensible,* whatever that means. Of course, we do live on a farm with miles of fences, with woods, streams, swamps, meadows, pastures, the whole nine yards. But I am not sure it would be all that different if we lived in an apartment. Well, perhaps not the cattle.

My son-the-doctor, Clay, and executive daughter, Pamela, and their chosen, Sheila and Joe (the matches are appropriate), are animal lovers. My two oldest grandchildren, Sarah and Joshua, have already shown themselves to be similarly afflicted and we have every reason to believe that the two youngest, Abaigeal [sic] and Hannah, will maintain the family tradition. It is going to be difficult for them if they don't! Anyway, it is out of the question. Not to worry. Quite unthinkable. Genes and environment, in this case, do conspire. Even psychologist B. F. Skinner would acknowledge the inevitability here.

As has been inevitable, I have lived, worked and played with animal enthusiasts of every stripe, hue, rosette and spot all of my adult life. The only club I have ever belonged to that I was able to maintain a really active interest in is the noble Westminster Kennel Club. To the other members of WKC I am sincerely grateful for not only grand fellowship lo these many dog-studded years, but for an ongoing education in matters canine. Where else can you find a Chet Collier, and until quite recently that ultimate gentleman, the late Bill Rockefeller, Bob Taylor, Bud McGivern, Ron Meneke, Bill Chisholm, Jim Stebbins, Fred Wagner, and their like all together in one room once a month?

Is there a difference between dog lovers, cat lovers, gorilla lovers, snake buffs or "herps," and elephant enthusiasts? Not as much as one might think. Often all those qualities (or afflictions) are found under one rib cage. People who have the ability to admire the beauty of, and have a sense of wonder over, other kinds of creatures are somehow special. I think those who can't because they are locked up in some egocentric/love-only-my-own-kind prison tend to be mean-spirited. Surely I must confess that I have known some perfectly dreadful people who have been self-professed "animal-lovers," but that has not been the rule, not at all. And if pushed I will admit that it is possible to be a nice enough person without caring about animals, but that is most unusual. It is highly unlikely, in fact. It is almost a contradiction of terms.

Generally, or at least very often, people with a deep interest in animals are the best people around. They show that they are not only compassionate, usually, but that they are free spirits in a way not unlike that of the animals they care about. Animal lovers are typically not focused inward, or at least not quite so sharply focused on their own id, ego, superego, and memories of their own toilet training; they are generally not trying to find themselves. Are there exceptions? Of course there are, but it will often be found that the so-called exceptions are really closet egomaniacs using animals to boost their income, bolster up a dreary, sagging image of self, or to put on a show to prove themselves to be what they are not but for some reason are sure they would like to be. Having a top-winning show dog or a horse "in the money" is a status thing, after all, if that is what you need. Lots of people want to appear richer than they are or at least appear comfortable with their wealth, and animals, unfortunately, are good for that kind of nonsense. Horses, dogs, cats, they all play into the hands of the insecure.

People who see themselves or want others to picture them as back-to-earth types may put their money on prize cattle or the like (usually not on pigs—they hit too close to home), I really don't think any animal should be used in that way.

An interesting fact is that people often have dogs, no matter what other animals they have. Dogs should have nothing whatsoever to do with money, or "means," or status—not really. They have everything to do with "heart," whether poor, rich or neither. But dogs do go handsomely with cattle, sheep and horses. For the full spectrum of people who just might own other animals it still seems to mean something, to satisfy something, or to be significant if not terribly important, that somewhere nearby *a dog is listening.*

So, to all of the dogs that have listened to me in my life I am deeply grateful and not just in the context of this book. For far more than that. And to the friends and strangers who have written and told me how the canine connection has worked in their lives, I am grateful, too. Clearly, if I were to list them all this would be a phone directory instead of an essay. That isn't necessary. You know who you are. With your love you have been my teachers. I have tried to be an attentive student and what follows, I guess, is my term paper.

A postscript of sorts: It is difficult when thinking and writing about animals to avoid sounding anthropomorphic, even when you are trying to avoid it, even when you know better. That is never more true than when you are dealing with a critter as close to our core family as a dog. I know, I promise you I know, that dogs don't *know* and *think* in the way we do those things. Dogs do think, however, and they do feel, but the limits of those internal events are far from being understood or defined. All that insight is in the future; perhaps it will only come when we better understand how they work within our own heads and hearts. (If you doubt that, explain in fifty words or less how you think or remember or feel. Go look it up if you want to.)

At any rate, we'll deal with that as we move along. When I say, though, that a dog knows something, *I* do not know whether that knowledge is part of the animal's genetic package, behavior learned from other dogs, a result of independent study on the part of the individual dog, or whether it is the result of instruction from us. (Instruction from us is often largely nagging and whining rather than straight, intelligence guidance.) Top dog trainer Brian Kilcommons has often said that ninety percent of the dogs in America have grown up thinking that their name was "No!"

Another thing: dogs deserve something I call *appanage*. All animals do. The word *appanage* comes from the old French and once referred to provisions made for a younger son, one who was not going to inherit the throne, title, chateau, or vineyard. In time, however, the word, by then transported across the Channel and legitimately part of the English language, came to mean anything that could be claimed or assigned by custom or tradition or as an acknowledgment of natural necessity. It is a rightful endowment. There are things that dogs have assigned to them by custom and tradition in segments of our society, and dogs certainly have natural necessities. Hence, *appanage*, dogs' rightful endowment. Some people use the expression "animal rights," but that term has become so confrontational that its continued use is likely to be counterproductive.

James Stuart, Duke of Richmond and Lennox, by Sir Anthony van Dyck.

1

MAN AND DOG have been together for just about as long as the idea or perhaps fortuitous accident of domesticated animals has existed. The only animal that may have been domesticated earlier than the dog is the goat. It could not have been an organized plan or concept when it first began with either the dog or the goat because domestication involves gene manipulation by selective breeding. As clever as cave people obviously were required to be in order to survive in their hostile and difficult world, one of their weaker suits had to have been genetics. It is not really certain that they even made the nine-month connection in their own lives. Sex was probably more opportunistic then than now, if that is possible. Our early ancestors would not have been very much more clever about the two phenomena in animals than they were when they bedded each other, although with their canine companions they were dealing with an abbreviated period of only sixty-three days between happenings.

Just when the dog became a fixture in our lives is not clear, but it was probably sometime between one hundred and fifty and two hundred and fifty centuries ago. It was not a sudden event. No one recorded, *"This afternoon after the three o'clock herbal tea break Erguum Slurm, Ernox Sturtz and I took a little time off from flint-chipping and domesticated*

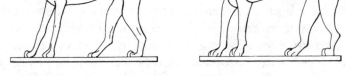

Four Egyptian dogs from the Twelfth Dynasty, c. 2000 B.C.

the dog." It was, rather, a long drawn-out affair, and although we are not sure where it happened, it probably was somewhere between present-day Israel and India. It was certainly before there were any designated states at all.

That vast and generally arid area is the range of a smallish wolf subspecies known as *Canis lupus pallipes*. It is believed that that wild canid was the principal ancestor of our domestic dog, *Canis domesticus*. Other forms of wolves would in time have input, but *pallipes* was probably the principal gene contributor. We'll discuss the dog's evolution in greater depth later, but, in short, the dog did not evolve from the wolf in a natural, orderly way. The dog was *extracted* from the wolf by man. We moved animals around and bred them by selecting for desirable characteristics. Much of it was, of necessity, hit or miss. There had to have been so much error that "trial-and-error" hardly seems to apply. We did ultimately select, though, for social instincts, apparently for intelligence and surely for temperament. It was all there waiting for us in the wolf and we dug it out over many centuries, perhaps as many as two hundred of them.

The domestication of animals can be viewed, one supposes, as just part of the deliberate exploitation of the environment by man. The only problem is that it probably wasn't all that deliberate. If ever there was serendipity, it was here in the great experiment of domestication. With some species, wild cattle for instance, it must have been very dangerous. With the wolf, though, man struck gold. Here were two species from very different parts of the mammalian family tree made for each other.

A draft evolutionary scenario is not without its difficulties. The remains of an obviously domesticated dog have been unearthed in a cave in Idaho! The bones date to about 8000 B.P. And the Plains Indians had dogs, too, far from any seaport. The dingo of Australia is feral, descended from domestic dogs of sorts and had to have been transported there a very long time ago. The mastiff was apparently developed in Tibet from heaven alone knows what ancestors and carried to Rome between two and three thousand years ago. Either there is something we don't know about the history of our dogs—multiple sites of domestication, for instance, and that seems at least possible—or an awful lot we don't know about the movement of our own ancestors. Dogs in England, Africa, Idaho, Australia, Mexico, Tibet, Siberia, and Borneo didn't just show up as strays coming in from the cold. They were either deliberate cottage-craft products or trade cargo or guards and

companions on voyages from who-knows-where by
who-can-tell-what-route conducted by who-knows, who-
can-say-when. More on all of this later.

What we do know—to backtrack a minute—is that by
a million years ago wolves were found over a vast range—
Ireland and Spain, through all of Europe, down through
the Indian subcontinent, all the way to Siberia and Japan,
and in North and Central America as well.

What all this means is that as man evolved there never
was a time and probably never a place where he wasn't
surrounded by wolves. The potential for extracting the
dog as a helper and probably before that as a companion
was there from the beginning. It is probable that by 20,000
years ago man had the dog underway and very shortly
after that would undertake the herding of ruminants using
dogs. That would have been 15,000 years ago.

Man would have already discovered that he was dealing
with an intelligent, social creature that he could relate to
with ease. Dogs, i.e., wolves, work together in major
hunting undertakings, just as man the domesticator was
learning to do when man and wolf first got together. It
was a natural symbiosis only, despite the common mis-
conception; both sides in a symbiotic relationship don't
have to gain equal benefits. It is not clear how the man-
wolf equation will work out and we'll discuss the evolution
of that equation more fully further on. But the most com-
plicating factor is that man dumped the wolf along the way
and from its residue created an entirely new species, the
domestic dog.

All of which leads us to the issue of breeding. As we
move along we will see the process of domestication develop, the change in body structure, face proportions, and
the reduction in brain size. All of that, apparently, is inevitable because it is seen in more than the wolf-to-dog
progression. All of the inbreeding and manipulation that
had to have been done first to achieve the basic dog and
then to slice it into 440 or so slices or "breeds" has had a

price. The dog has paid the piper with genetic faults and
potential health problems, an extended discussion of which
we'll deal with in the last chapter of this book.

So where does all of this leave us? For one thing, it allows
us to understand our dogs through their ancestral wolves.
We are dealing with an animal equipped with the wolfish
instincts needed for social structure, dominance, hierar-
chies, and, without question, communication. Canines
that live and hunt together, wolf or dog, must be able to
communicate during the cooperative effort if they are to
feed themselves and their young and, as importantly, during mating time and cub rearing, when dominance, instruction in the complex art of staying alive, and territory
are factors. Powerful animals that live, travel, and hunt
together either have to communicate with each other or
fight. Dominance has to be established and maintained
without constantly being tested with fangs and teeth. It
has to be asserted with signals, not blood, and that is
equally true of submission. In animals as formidable as
wolves fighting would eventually prove to be the mark of
an unsuccessful species. The outcome within a social pack
would have to be terrible.

Wolf cubs and dog pups are not precocious. As with
most highly intelligent species—elephants, whales, apes,
human beings, and cats are other examples—there has to
be a long tutorial period. Good tutors, i.e., parents, have
to be able to communicate with their young, and the young
have to be really good listeners and observers or they will
never be able to survive once they are off on their own.
That is axiomatic. Pay attention or perish.

The forward movement from newborn to mature animal
is an inexorable process, relentless. Eventually every animal surviving the early stages of its development matures
enough to be forced away from the parental shield. (One
of the distinctions in the redefinition of man suggested by
Louis Leakey could accurately be stated that we are indeed
the only species equipped with apron strings!) The sepa-

Brand new.

Two days old, eyes not open.

First steps out into the world.

ration must happen largely because the parent, usually only one parent, the mother, wants to get on with life, mate again, and have more young. That is the demand made by the species striving toward its ultimate goal, survival. Relatively few species keep young of different age groups together for long. We do, apes and elephants do, and there are others, of course, but most species don't find it a good survival tactic. For one thing, it could increase the danger of inbreeding, parents mating with their own offspring and half- or full-brothers and sisters with each other. (We'll focus more on inbreeding toward the end of the book.)

When the time comes for the young to go off on their own, the separation becomes a terrible test for predators, a gauntlet that must be run. Only those species whose members have been able to learn their survival skills well enough to pass them along to their own young can survive. No wild species can allow very many dolts to survive long enough to breed. In hunting animals it is most important because, unlike herbivores, they can't just drop their heads and graze or lift them and browse.

Hunting is a complex and often extremely hazardous occupation, a very hard way to make a living. Some prey animals kick, almost all bite, many scratch, some gore, others crush and not just a few envenomate. A hunting animal cannot hope to survive the challenges it is destined to face again and again unless it has done its homework, unless it has listened. Luck is a thin thread to hang from when you are hungry or your offspring are.

As formidable as the behavior of animals that don't want to be eaten may be, starvation is an even greater threat. Carrion is all right when it is available, but sooner or later killing is necessary for all of the true predators. That, with wolves, is where cooperation and communication come in. Packs usually don't carry dead weight around for very long, and animals that can't work in concert and play their part when the moment of truth is at hand are dead weights. (That is not inevitably the case, however. Few things in the nature of the beast are. For two years we observed a three-legged lioness in Ngorongoro Crater in Tanzania. Clearly she was a dead weight and couldn't have hunted for herself, but the members of her pride obviously let her utilize their kills and protected her for the years that she did live. A hyena apparently got her leg when she was a cub and likely took the rest of her when she was between four and five. There are an enormous number of hyenas in the Crater and they are always on the lookout for gifts from heaven like three-legged lionesses.)

In their wolf incarnation our pets and companions had to remain alert to opportunity if they were to survive as hunters. In both North America and Europe herds of bison were preyed upon by wolves and their approach in the thousands would send out thunderous noise and earth-thudding signals. In the Far North today caribou and reindeer (actually the same species) also move in large numbers and are hunted by wolves along their migratory routes.

Any number of hoofed animals moved through the world of *C. l. pallipes* in substantial herds while packs of waiting predators listened for the sounds of many animals on the move, sensing it through the ground.

Even wolves hunting for individual prey and not seeking vast herds must depend on their ears as prime gatherers of data. I have never heard a discussion of the chances a deaf wolf would have in the wild but I suspect they would not be very good. Nature is terribly intolerant of imperfection, as indeed she must be. It is one of the biggest favors she can do for a species, keeping them honed.

Besides thumping and thundering along, animals make other sounds predators can rely on. Young animals bawl and bleat, yawn aloud, suckle, squeak, squabble and sniffle. Males of many species clash horns and antlers and thump heads in play or in earnest hierarchal displays and contests during breeding season. Animals sip, suck, hum, purr, groan, slurp, and splash in water, rub against vegetation, send pebbles and rocks rolling over cliffs and down hill-

sides, pull down branches, and snip twigs. They call to each other, cough, snort, pant, wheeze, sneeze, and argue. Animals scratch to counter external parasites, and that can be downright noisy if the listener has good ears. The intestinal activity of a great many animals makes a whole concert of sounds. That repertoire is collectively known as borborygmus and can be virtually symphonic in volume and complexity among bovids with a cluster of stomachs. Wolves and dogs use their noses to a large extent when hunting, it is true, and some forms have astounding eyesight, but always, without fail, they listen. A snapping twig, a passing of gas, this moment's overheard biological trivia could become the source of a meal in a matter of minutes.

What else might a dog living under wild conditions listen for? Warnings, certainly. As we have suggested, fighting among large carnivores is not desirable and usually can be avoided by submission, respect for territory and other social devices, matters all ethologically derived. Growls, grumbling, whining, yapping, howling, gnashing teeth— all of these sounds constitute a dialogue of sorts, and although we, as students of our companion animals, are taught what some of the signals mean, we hardly understand them all. What matters is that our pets do. They listen to each other. That is one way they have evolved to get along. As social animals, wolves move in groups, packs, or hunting parties. Listening to each other, especially when it is dark or the forest is thick, could help coordinate movement. It could, certainly does, help keep youngsters under control.

We can see this interchange at work in our domestic dogs. Anyone who has watched a bitch tend to her litter has seen a remarkable display of vocal communication. (The temptation to say "verbal" is almost overwhelming, but that would probably be overdoing it and I must not press my luck.) Most female dogs decide by the time their pups are weaned that the whole thing was a terrible mistake, the worst idea they ever had. It is instructive how the bitches make that clear to their offspring. They generally don't actually bite their puppies, but they certainly can be convincing that they intend to. And the puppies listen. (Hey, I listen when a dog growls at me!)

A notable exception to the child-rejection syndrome was

observed in a beautiful and gentle female bloodhound
named Trinity. She was the broodiest animal I have ever
met. A champion of record at ten months, she was about
as beautiful as a bloodhound can get, laid back, a perfect
lady in all respects. When her puppies arrived she was
attentive and always showed deep concern for their wel-
fare. The strange thing was that when the time came to
get the puppies onto solid food Trinity did none of the
warning-away things other bitches just naturally do. We
kept two of the puppies and sold the other eight, and even
when those two puppies were as big as she was (the male,
in fact, grew to be much larger), she worried about them
day and night. If they tussled and made squealing noises
she flew to them and examined them for signs of injury.
She slept with one eye and both ears open. She listened
for the slightest sound of distress. It was an amazing display
of an instinctive pattern that wouldn't turn off. Some hor-
mone or other didn't swing into action on schedule. She
never did stop listening for their calls until her own death,
sadly, at four and a half. She was that highest of high-risk
bloodhounds, a rock-eater. One too many rocks finally
got her and even extensive surgery couldn't repair the dam-
age she had done to herself. She developed gangrene of
the intestines. But to the end her puppies had her full
attention.

There are certain obvious sounds that all members of
the dog family must monitor which reveal the connection
between the predatory instincts of wolves and the nature
of our pets. Footsteps that can be detected either as airborne
sounds or ground vibrations that are a mix of actual
sounds, and a thumping sensation underfoot are clear examples. Remember the herds of bison the wolves hunted?

We keep horses around our place because they look
lovely grazing on the hillsides, because we like the way
they smell, and because they are pleasant animals we find
it easy to relate to as overgrown companions of sorts. But
mostly we have horses because our own now-grown chil-

dren and their kids like to drop over and either saddle up
or hitch up.

When horses feel chipper because of a change in the
temperature or perhaps because they have picked up on
some signal we would naturally miss, they will often kick
out at nothing in particular and go galloping off across the
meadow. They obviously feel good about it because horses
love to run. It is what they are all about. We enjoy the
sight of manes and tails blowing in the wind, even if the
wind is generated by the horses themselves. It is a pretty
thing to see, and although the expression has been over-
used, it is poetry in motion.

We have a border collie named Duncan. His father,
Mike, is quite a famous dog. Mike's owner and trainer,
Clint Rowe, the man who gave us Duncan, has put Mike
in heaven-alone-knows how many television commercials
and trained him to star in *Down and Out in Beverly Hills*.
It is not every dog you can look at and say, *"His father
peed on Bette Midler's rug."* There is a tone to that, a certain
ring. After all, how many times can you use your dog for
name dropping?

Duncan has extremely acute hearing. Perhaps that is bred
into borders because in their native Scotland shepherds
signal their dogs with soft whistles and words as well as
with hand movements. Border collies are always on duty,
always listening. No matter where Duncan is, no matter
which way he is facing, when the horses get frisky he is
off like a shot, running to and eventually with the great
thundering beasts. We can't seem to break him of the habit.
When he hears those vibrations through the ground or the
air he is hostage to all of his genes. Clint told me that even
the superbly trained Mike had to get his leg broken running
after horses before he learned his lesson. We know Duncan
has to get his sooner or later. Harsh as it may seem, I will
settle for a broken leg. Sheba, one of the thundering herd,
is a draft horse and weighs as much as thirty-five border
collies, at least. She could put Duncan over the barn if she

ever caught him squarely with even one hoof. But that sound, or probably those sounds, when they come to Duncan in any weather, no matter where he is on the farm, signals a dog possessed. If he is in the house, or up in the kennels with me in my office, he begs to be let out and answer the call of his destiny. Running animals are electric to him, but that isn't what is so interesting. What is astounding is how acutely he hears them, how he is always listening, how quickly he reacts. I don't think Duncan ever stops listening for footsteps or hoofbeats.

We have several other breeds of dogs as well. You will get to meet the wonderful giant droolers, the bloodhounds, the splendid, always accommodating greyhounds, the basset, the petite basset griffon vendeen and the pug. My granddaughter's Labrador, Zack, is also frequently about the place wagging up a storm, pleased with everybody and everything, and so is Annie, her Jack Russell terrier, and her greyhound, Luke. All of these dogs, like all self-respecting dogs, enjoy a good woof-up or yapping bee when vehicles come down the drive, but they all almost inevitably take their signal from Duncan whose ears are on twenty-four-hour duty. He has to be really away on the other side of the marsh or deep in the woods not to be the first to report that our perimeter has been compromised.

Our driveway is long and cars do not come roaring down toward the house. As soon as a car turns off the road the signs start warning drivers to slow down because of children, horse-drawn vehicles, and resident animals. Visitors generally comply and come creeping down between the barn and the kennels.

Duncan can be asleep on a carpeted floor on one of three levels in the house, shielded from any imaginable vibrations, but he hears tires crunching the stone and earth in the driveway as soon as a vehicle leaves the tarmac and turns in to Thistle Hill Farm—and he goes on instant red alert. His hearing is uncanny. Naturally, as soon as Duncan gives the alarm, some or most of the other dogs join in pretending that they heard the intruders first. They generally look a little embarrassed about not really having been the first to know.

There have been occasions when Duncan was so worn out from trying to catch the greyhounds doing their laps that Amelia the pug actually has been the initial alarm-sounder. When that has happened Duncan has regained consciousness with a terrible start. He hates to be caught off guard. He seems to know his hearing is the most acute around and he appears to take pride in being first with the news.

Reggie, our oldest greyhound, does not participate. He has a different agenda and probably feels that if ten or so other dogs are barking he could contribute little or no meaningful additional information. I don't think I have ever heard him really bark, in fact, but he does listen. You can see him doing it. He gets a look in his eyes when the ten-dog crescendo begins. It is a look asking if anybody really needs him for anything or if it is all right for him to go back to sleep. Reggie would much rather sleep than bark any day. He is the ultimate couch potato. Since he came off the track, we feel it is his right.

We do not have one dog that I can even imagine biting anyone, although Sirius (or Xyreus) (we will be getting to him) tends to give people a start. It is not a threat display when the dogs, generally picking up on Duncan's cue, sound off. It is a response to the certain knowledge that dogs have that everybody in the family pack is listening. We expect our dogs to listen to us when we speak to them and our dogs, no less than we, do expect us to listen to them. When Duncan barks, when the others join in, we are witnessing communication at work. The subject, of course, is territory, a subject dogs, like a great many other animals, take very seriously. Dogs probably "talk" about territory more than they do about any other single subject. It should be noted, however, that ethologists, students of the evolution of behavior, are not really comfortable with

*Top, Greek lamp (400 B.C.), a greyhound with a hare in its mouth.
Bottom, a greyhound as drinking horn (300 B.C.).*

generalized statements about why dogs bark. It remains, apparently, all rather speculative, although some of the reasons seem pretty clear to me.

When dogs bark at an approaching stranger they are not necessarily all communicating the same thing. As soon as Duncan knows that we have the message and his responsibility has been fulfilled, he stops. He is not a yapper. He is simply telling us that he has received a message from tires or footsteps that he feels obligated to pass along. Amelia, on the other hand—like Winnie, another pug who was gathered many years ago, and Brigitte, a toy poodle that has also gone on ahead—keeps the thing going even

after the people have been received at the door, even after
they are in the house, unless she is commanded to stop in
a convincingly authoritarian tone. What stops Amelia
quicker than anything else is acknowledgment. Amelia demands attention when we are invaded, Duncan simply calls
it to our attention.

The other dogs seem to be doing a choral kind of thing.
If it is a cool, sunny day the bloodhounds may move their
deep, heavy bark up a notch and yodel. Lizzie the basset
thinks that is a grand idea and sings along with the best
of them. Anyone who has heard hounds singing has had
to be thrilled by it. It takes one back to much earlier times
in our history and is quite as wonderful musically as the
incredible songs of wolves and coyotes. I am not sure what
it all means. It could be territorial (that may be one of the
principal reasons wolves sing at dusk). Perhaps the hounds,
certain that everyone will listen, send forth their great bale-
ful song to establish and identify turf, or perhaps it is just
to proclaim the joy and glory of self. It may be both because
there is obviously joy in turf and a fuller sense of self. I
know I feel very differently about a farm that I own than
I did about an apartment I once rented. (I know, I *know*,
only man has an awareness of self, according to that earlier
definition of man. But humor me, please.)

So those are some of the more obvious imperatives that
keep wolves and dogs listening: food, the need to anticipate
and locate prey, inter-pack warnings centering on intruders
who may be bad news in the pack's territory, and demands
for structure within the pack itself. Both structure and
territory are essential elements in wolf life, and by natural
extension, in dog life. There is, too, the need for females
to monitor their young. All of these things are best done
by listening, and that is what both wolves and dogs do,
all the time.

2

How well do dogs hear? Very well, indeed. But first, of course, the inevitable comparison. Actually, it is our baseline. How well do we hear?

Sound as we perceive it is expressed in cycles per second—cps—which are actually vibrations per second in a rapidly repetitive format. As adults, those of us (*you,* actually—I have a wonky left ear) who have not been handicapped by an insult (like a grenade going off nearby, or a position in a rock band near the speakers, or in front of the percussion instruments) or disease, hear from a low of about twenty cps (a tuba with a sore throat) to a high of about twenty thousand. As small children we probably functioned up in the forty thousand cps range, but time does take its toll. The eardrum thickens as we age and the small bones inside of the ear that transmit the vibrations become less responsive. It has been suggested that by the time we reach our forties (which by my present reckoning is late childhood) we probably lose as much as eighty cps's worth of sensitivity every six months. That would be natural attrition, not anything pathological.

And the rest of the animal kingdom? How sensitive are other species to sound? A mouse hears up to ninety-five thousand cycles, easily, at least. Little wonder cats walk gingerly on padded feet. Bats operate in that range, too,

or higher, probably one hundred and twenty thousand cps
when they are echolocating during flight in reduced light.
The astounding thing is that the echoes coming back to
the swiftly flying bat dashing and dodging around its own
air space may exert no more than 1/10,000 of the pressure
contained in the sound sent forth by the little animal a
fraction of a second before. Still, the bat can detect it and
use it to home in on prey as small as flying insects and to
avoid things as large as church steeples and human hair
styles (in which they do *not* become entangled).

Crickets and grasshoppers stridulate from a low of four
thousand cps to one hundred thousand, but the range apparently varies considerably from species to species, which
may be one reason why we don't find cricket-grasshopper
crosses in our meadows. Like the FCC, nature has assigned
bands to her species and given them their own aerial territory to use for establishing social opportunities. Rats are
thought to operate at around forty thousand cps, just about
where we did as small children when we were generally
startled and frightened by sudden or loud noises. Porpoises
are probably the all-time champions, utilizing a range up
to a hundred and fifty thousand cycles—seven and a half
times our top range as adults. Now, that is listening! (Imagine having that kind of hearing and a whiny child or nagging spouse!) Our companion cats hear up to fifty thousand
cycles. All wild felines are thought to have very acute
hearing. Since cats often operate after dark, they depend
heavily on their acute hearing, as do owls. After all, how
noisy is a mouse on a hardwood floor? How loudly does
a sparrow snore?

Compared to us, then (but not necessarily to the rest of
the animal kingdom), dogs have phenomenal hearing. We
believe that they utilize sound up to about thirty-five thousand cycles. By *utilize* it is meant that they can hear and
identify sound at that high frequency—whichever it is—
and probably communicate up there with some of their
musical gyrations. The incredible musical wizard, Paul

Winter, has used actual wolf howls (as well as whale songs) in his compositions for years and I have heard him *ooh* and *aah* over the things the wild canids were doing musically, picking up on each other's notes, for example, and all of that just within the range of Paul's ultrasensitive but inevitably human ears. What the wolves might be doing in the fifteen or eighty thousand cycles beyond Paul's hearing is anybody's guess. They could have all kinds of concerts up in that stratospheric range without Paul or anyone else being able to pick up on them.

There are some reports of research in Russia indicating that dogs may, in fact, hear in the hundred thousand cycle range, almost three times that which has generally been thought to be the top of their top. We don't know very much about that, yet, or why they would need it and what it would do to help explain them as complete animals. In this book we will march on, considering dogs as thirty-five-thousand-cycle animals.

The dogs of the world have a whole universe of sound far beyond our reach. Much of what we don't understand about them may go on up there while we struggle down

here below trying to interpret them and their purposes in terms of what we hear and then can know. It is a little like trying to understand the fuss made over Monet or Van Gogh if you have been color-blind from birth. (Go on— try to describe what color is like to someone who has always lacked the essential rod-and-cone combination to perceive it.)

Two things about the hearing range of dogs and of any other species, for that matter. There are two different range requirements. Insofar as dogs communicate with each other, and they do, there must be some kind of match-up between the sounds emitted and the sounds perceived within the species. Since dogs may cut off up around thirty-five thousand cycles (let's forget about that one hundred thousand cycle possibility for the moment), there wouldn't seem to be much sense in yowling at each other or anything else at twice that level. That would really have them howl-ing at the moon. It would be a waste of energy and talent, and nature is always impatient with waste.

The second consideration concerns dogs/wolves as eavesdroppers. They have to be able to hear the sounds made by other animals. Other animals could be enemies and, in the case of the wolf, they could be brunch. In either case, it serves the purposes of survival to be able to keep a running check on ambient biological static. Any animal in the thirty-five cps range hears plenty of such static all of the time. And we have no way of knowing how well they are able to filter out the unneeded or unwanted sounds. I do know that even the most acutely aware dogs can sleep so soundly you have to do everything but douse them with a bucket of cold water to get their attention. Duncan, our border collie, for example, has to be called three or four times when he is herding the sheep of his dreams (dogs *do* dream), but, a grunch of footsteps or tires in the driveway or running horses in the farthest pasture from the house generally has him off like a mortar shell in ascendancy. That would seem to suggest that a dog can drop off to sleep leaving certain channels open and others off. We don't really know that, however. In observing animal behavior, essentially an anecdotal experience, it is not clear how much can be extracted from empirical observation without the advantage of theory or a discernible system.

It would seem, then, that there have been two imperatives in the evolution of the dog's ear, and it is not an easy determination to say which has been the more important, if indeed either has, which I doubt. Matching the range in their own unique social context would enable them to be successful parents, hunters, and guardians of territory, while being able to locate and interpret prey would lead to the same end. Two, imperatives, yes, but in parallel and with a common goal. (Actually, evolution doesn't have varying goals, as such, but rather, results. The goal for all species in all circumstances is the same— survival.)

The dog brings the same kind of ear power and the traces of both imperatives down from the world of the wolf into our shared households. That explains why dogs listen to us. We are their pack, now, and they listen to us so that we may all get on together, the way wolves do. Our dogs also listen because although they are probably not hunting their own food for a living, the instinct is there for territorial integrity and for lots of other reasons the dogs themselves, I am sure, could never now understand.

All of this instinctive pressure has turned our dogs into incurable busybodies. They look, but mostly they listen around corners, down staircases, near windows, under dining room and kitchen tables. They like being with us, it is true—they are very social, after all—but they also like to have a vantage point and to be up on all of the latest gossip. They are collectors of trivia. Imagine, though, how frustrating it must be for them when we sit by the phone and drone on and on without their being able to understand the words or comprehend what if any relationships exist

to justify so much sound. We do tend to talk in something of a monotone when we are on the phone, unless someone has called to tell us we have won the lottery. Chatting up a handful of plastic must seem a silly thing to them. But that isn't a bad thing. Trying to understand us has to be one of the dog's most diverting recreations.

How is a dog's ear constructed? Meticulously. It was evolved to function full-time and to serve many purposes. The part you see when you look at your dog is generally called the pinna. That pinna, made of auricular cartilage covered with skin, and generally hairier on the outside than on the inside, has a whole battery of names and designations. It is also called the leather, the meatus and the lobe, and is known in its many styles. There are bat ears and tulip ears, bear or blunt-tipped ears, button and candle-flame, as well as cocked or semi-drop ears. There are also drop or dropped ears, erect ears, filbert ears, flop ears, fly or flying ears, heart-shaped ears, high set and hooded ears, hound, curled-in and lobe or lobular ears, pendant, pendulous, prick, or pricked, and propeller ears. There are rolled ears, rose ears, sharp-tipped and triangular ears, and trowel ears, too. There are v-shaped ears and even some known as vine-leaf.

The junction of the pinna or earlobe base and the skull is known as the set-on. That set-on, specific in style to the different breeds of dogs, is important in more places than the show ring. The set-on and all the minute muscles that control the movement of the pinna help the dog express itself. Watch your dog and see how much you can interpret from the ears. We think of the ear as an organ of hearing and balance, not as a means of expression. That is because few of us do anything interesting with our pinnas, but our dogs do. The difference between a lick and a bite is generally foretold by ear set and movement, for those who care to look.

The auricular cartilage, whatever its shape, rolls into a tube as it approaches the skull and drops down vertically as the first stage of the ear canal. At some point it turns to the horizontal and goes in to meet the eardrum, or tympanic membrane. Our ear canal, for comparison, has no vertical part, it just goes horizontally in to the ear drum. That is why it is safer to clean your dog's ears than it is your own.

Once the pinna has channeled incoming vibrations (sounds) down the outer-ear canal and they have taken that hard right turn they encounter the eardrum. From there they are transmitted into the middle ear or tympanic cavity or bulla, where they are picked up by a series of three bones or auditory ossicles, the hammer, the sickle, and the anvil. After transmission by the three bones through the middle ear they hit the oval window and pass into the third and last chamber, the inner ear. Once there, a device known as the cochlea converts what up to now have been mechanical stimuli into nerve impulses. Those impulses move up the auditory nerves to the brain for interpretation, at which point it can be said that the dog has heard. But back a step so we can better understand this remarkable

device called the ear. As the mechanical vibrations pass
through the oval window into the inner ear and the cochlea,
they stimulate a series of structures—the utricle and the
vestibular semicircular ducts, or canals, as they are sometimes known. Those devices enable dogs to maintain their
balance, and although dogs do not generally climb up trees,
roofs, and chicken coops, and get themselves into the pre-
carious situations our cats do, they still need to have four
feet under them when they want them there. Dogs have
an absolute dread of losing their balance. Falling down is
far more than embarrassing for our dogs, it is terrifying.

So, then, those simple-appearing flaps of skin, whatever
their shape or posture, play many roles. They help give
dogs a hearing range far above our own adult range, as
expressed in cycles per second, they allow the dog to remain properly oriented toward the planet, and they have
a language of their own that helps keep the social glue of
the wolf/dog firm. It is perhaps ironic that the external
devices dogs use for hearing are at the same time the source
of a very critical means of visual communication.

In at least one set of highly specialized desert cultures,
an adjustment is made to guarantee good hearing. Dogs
are regarded as little better than vermin in the world of
Islam, except for the saluki and to some limited extent
other sight hounds derived from the saluki and the greyhound. That does not stop the pragmatic desert tribes from
using dogs as guards for their flocks. To make certain their
dogs stay alert, they cut off the dogs' pinnas. The ear canal
is then unprotected from buzzing flies and other flying
insects, so the dogs remain irritable and awake. It is an
infuriating thing to see, but, alas, you cannot travel in Arab
lands without encountering the practice. Any suggestion
to the locals that the dog deserves better at our hands would
draw blank stares.

The price of domestication can be high. I know of no
studies that would tell us how many wolves are born deaf
but some breeds of dogs have had deafness built into their

genes, undoubtedly by our mucking about with their DNA. As a result, the potential for that handicap is always there. No less than fifteen of the 130 or so breeds recognized by the American Kennel Club have deafness listed as a hereditary or congenital disease. They are the American as well as the English foxhound, the Australian shepherd, Boston terrier, bull terrier, collies, both the rough and smooth, dachshunds (smooth, long-haired, and wire-haired), dalmatian, English setter, fox terrier, Great Dane, Great Pyrenees, Maltese, and Scottish terrier. How often deafness occurs in each breed is not a matter of record and since breeders are likely to keep such problems in their own lines private we may never know. It is a problem from birth, however, and can be determined at an age of seven to ten days when a puppy's ears are scheduled to go on line as a functional sense. It is not something that is likely to show up later, not if it is congenital.

Sound can be measured in other ways, too, not just in frequency. There is the matter of volume. Sound at any frequency can be loud or soft, come from near or far. Hunters who are in the field a lot with their dogs say their

dogs can hear sounds much too low in volume for human ears to detect. There are instances where dogs have been reported picking up the sounds of waterfowl calling to each other or landing on water over half a mile away. I personally have heard sandhill cranes bugling high in the sky, but the giant birds were directly overhead and the sounds they produced were pouring down on us and were loud enough even at that distance to produce ripples in a lake. (Not literally, a mere figure of speech for emphasis.) Those same sounds coming across a field, through tall grass and reeds, through trees, over varying terrain, would probably not have been detectable by me. Apparently, though, they could have been by dogs.

Consider the value of that enlarged sensitivity. The farther away a sound is when it is detected, the longer the time the wolf/dog has to decipher it and muster defenses within his own social unit or organize a hunting party if the sounds suggest prey. The position the pinna is in when a distant sound is detected can contribute a direction-finding ability. By turning his body position, listening intently while changing the position and attitude of the pinna, the wolf/dog can react to the volume and nature of the vibrations being directed against the eardrum for eventual translation into impulses to the brain. The ear's task is to track and gather the sound but, again, the ear interprets nothing, gives no commands. All of those higher functions happen at the far end of the auditory nerve. If other senses are involved at the same time, smell and sight being most likely, the brain will sort out all of that simultaneously and give the dog a series of commands based on all incoming data. There is an incredible random-wired computer involved. By the intensity of its concentration the dog can feed in (and up) the greatest amount of data in the fastest way possible and have the shortest lag between delivering the data and getting the appropriate marching orders. Those orders frequently spell the difference between life and death.

Many dogs find loud noises difficult to deal with. Some people I know had a massive black Newfoundland that pulled a cart with kids in it and even gave rides like a pony. He was a quiet, reasonable giant in all things except thunderstorms when he went absolutely crazy. It has never been really clear to me whether dogs that appear to be especially sensitive to thunder really are, or are just reacting badly to low barometric pressure conditions that prevail when electrical storms occur. There might be other clues, too, that dogs worry about. The smell of ozone from lightning, for example. I opt for the sound factor, although clearly dogs could well detect low pressure conditions and predict the coming thunder and the discomfort it causes them. They would know from experience. If a dog's mother had been especially sensitive, it could have learned to fear the sounds even if they did not cause them physical pain. It is difficult to sort such things out.

My dog-trainer friend Brian Kilcommons capitalizes on how sensitive dogs are to sudden, loud nosies. He takes an empty metal coffee can, puts a few coins in it, and then tapes the plastic top back on. When a dog is misbehaving (stealing food off a kitchen counter, for instance), he throws the can near (not at!) the dog and shouts a negative command: *"No!"* *"Out!"* *"Leave it!"*—something like that. The sudden noise, reinforced by a negative voice tone, generally does the trick quickly. Dogs hate sudden noise almost as much as they hate losing their footing. Dog trainers keep those things in mind.

Anyway, back to the great black Newf. When he discerned a storm coming he inevitably headed for home where he obviously felt safer than anywhere else. For better or worse, my friends allowed their giant pet the freedom to wander their suburban neighborhood, not generally a wise idea. But Olaf was altered, he wasn't a fighter (he just drooled more when he felt stressed), and he appeared to have better-than-average road sense. One day he was apparently a little slow in picking up the advance warnings;

either that or the storm system moved in too fast for him to respond to it in advance.

Olaf was not home when the first thunder cracked down from the heavens like the vengeance of hell. He apparently freaked. He was crossing a neighbor's front yard when the insult to his nervous system occurred and he went through an eight-foot-wide picture window, scattering buckets of glass on two tables' worth of ladies having a bridge party. He passed under both card tables and across the top of a refreshment-laden coffee table, heading for the kitchen where he completed his remarkable performance by going clean through a glass kitchen door. He never broke stride. He was somewhat disruptive to the card games and to trays of finger sandwiches. (It had hardly been worth the trouble to cut the crusts off the bread or even devil the eggs.)

My friends' neighbors were not amused. My friends quietly paid for the damages. One suspects Olaf had a headache, he didn't say, but not a cut did he have. And this was not special-effects glass made of sugar that people and animals go through in the movies. This was *glass* glass!

Other friends had a vizsla who performed in reverse. During an electrical storm he went *out* through a picture window. He needed stitches. In this particular case that was one of the least destructive things the dog did during his long career. Still, they loved Bela despite the fact that he bit me. Perhaps that is why they liked him. One never knows. A dog that bites may be an extension of the unconscious or at least hidden mind of the owner. I tend to blame owners for my scar tissue. I find it difficult to blame dogs for very much.

I don't know whether acute sensitivity to loud noises like thunder and gunfire (sirens and firecrackers) goes with particularly acute hearing or whether it has to do with other factors. It is often suggested that sirens set some dogs (certainly not all) to howling because the shrieking hurts those particular dogs' ears. It is often said that dogs howl

when the fire trucks go by because of the musical training
of their genes. A wailing tone, rising and falling with the
Doppler effect, becomes a wolf on a distant hill in the
ancient memories all sentient species realize, I am sure. I
don't know how to sort that out.

Our border collie, Duncan, who is curled up next to me
and oblivious to his incipient fame even as I write this is
very much affected for the worse by loud noises. At the
first sign of an electrical storm everybody rushes around
the house calling to each other in near-hysteria, "Where is
Duncan?" If he is not in the house he will inevitably be

found cowering near the back door with a glazed look in his eyes. That is, if he is located before the heavenly bowling balls get close. If he is not in (and like Olaf the Newf he heads for home when he senses what I am certain is a drop in barometric pressure) and the thunder gets going, he is gone, mindlessly running in any direction he happens to be facing. After a thunderstorm we have found him cowering on a strange farm miles away. He becomes all unglued. He is extremely well trained in almost all things, but not when the gnomes of noise get going in the sky.

Inadvertently, I once sent Duncan off on one of his wild dashes when the sky was clear and the sun bright. After three particularly irksome phone conversations in a row (things do come in bunches) I sought to ease inner tensions by having do at a couple of paper targets and some tin cans. I have always done a fair amount of target shooting, although turning a firearm on anything that is breathing would be about as far from recreation as I think it would be possible to get. On this particular day I selected a .357 Magnum to express my mood. Although not exactly a "plinker" because of the cost of ammunition, a .357 certainly makes good emotional punctuation marks. I can't honestly say that I see my tormentors out there sitting cross-legged on the three posts of my revolver's sights, but something like that, on a subliminal level, probably does go on. I tend to leave that kind of reflection alone. Whatever works for you, as the kids today say.

So be it. I was busy sending tin cans in all directions and with great satisfaction punching neat wad-cutter holes in the eight, nine and ten circles on a paper target without realizing that Duncan was not only in the next county but the next state. Literally, we retrieved him from Pennsylvania, and we live in Maryland. Since that day, the first thing anyone on this farm does before going plinking is find Duncan and put him in the house or kennel, as far away from the noise as possible.

3

O BVIOUSLY dogs register the details of their world through more channels than just their two ears. Like all the rest of their fellow mammals they are presumed to have at least the five universally acknowledged senses. We will come to the obviously qualifying *at least* further along in our deliberations. We will suggest that to settle for that as their complete sensory array is far short of the mark. However, they are equipped to receive sound, sight, smell, taste, and touch. But those five inputs alone wouldn't come close to explaining observable canine behavior. First, though, we should deal with the remainder of the Big Five. From pinna, then, to pupil.

Sight? A to Z. Some dogs have very good eyesight and the ability to put that gift to work. The list would include the retrievers and the so-called sight or gaze hounds. The latter group are the descendants of ancient salukis and greyhounds, both very much still with us, as well as some breeds that are now surely extinct. Other dogs tend to use their eyes less than others and probably have relatively dismal sight.

The eye of the dog is pretty much the garden-variety mammalian eye. It is close to round and has a light-sensitive membrane lining the rear of the ball called the retina. There, incoming light is focused and information

assembled is sent to central control via the substantial optic nerve. It is a very rapid sequence of events, happening in a fraction of a second when the situation demands instantaneous response. Since dogs have two eyes, the standard, they do have binocular vision. They wouldn't be able to hunt without it. When looking straight ahead, the dog's field of vision overlaps. The greater the overlap, the greater the ability to judge depth, and therefore the distance between objects, animate or otherwise, in the foreground and the background. Binocular vision also provides the ability to discern details that aid in recognition.

There is the perhaps apocryphal story of a Stone Age tribe of people found in the deep forests on one of the myriad Philippine islands. They had never come out of the forest, at least in the memory of any living member. Some were brought out shortly after they were discovered. They stood aghast looking out over an expanse of rice paddies. What they saw, since they had had no experience with open areas and therefore distance, were human beings and water buffalo the size of toy soldiers. The figures they were seeing were far away, but *far away* was not something they had ever experienced. In short order their eyes and brain adjusted to the reality of size and distance, but it evidently caught them up short at first. Translate that phenomenon to the world of the wolf/dog. Without the ability to judge perspective—theirs because their two eyes' fields of vision overlap in the middle—the wolf or dog hunter would simply not be able to stalk, kill, or survive.

The dog has a total visual field of two hundred and fifty degrees. Depending on the kind of face we have created for the different breeds, the area of overlap or binocular vision ranges from about seventy-five degrees for long-nosed dogs to eighty-five degrees for short-nosed breeds, pugs over borzois. For comparison, humans have about one hundred and twenty degrees of binocular vision. But we have a total visual field of only one hundred and ninety degrees, which means dogs have sixty degrees more peripheral vision than we do. That suits our respective lifestyles. Peripheral vision is invaluable for a hunter trying to feed himself by making a kill, while the ability to focus on details (thanks to binocular vision) helps watchmakers, stamp collectors, and accountants. That is what evolution is all about. It is not a plan but a response. In return, in man and dog, we each have become what our sensory package has allowed us to evolve into. Evolution, in that sense, is a hoop rolling forward through time. In both of our species our senses have evolved into what we needed them to be in order for us to survive and we in turn have evolved into creatures that can utilize the worlds our senses have opened up for us.

The dog's eye is smaller than ours and although the cells in the retina of man and dog are the same size, only about seventy-five percent of the image we perceive emerges from the dog's retina for interpretation by his brain. The dog, seeing less detail than we do, is thus hampered when what he is looking at is stationary. Dogs (like many other animals) seek corroboration for what they think their eyes see, unless the subject is moving. Dogs are alert to movement, can perceive direction, speed, and trajectory when that is a factor, and can probably recognize familiar animal species from patterns of movement. They may even be able to recognize familiar individuals, you for example, by the way you walk. Like most hunters, at least mammalian hunters, wolves and dogs as well, almost certainly can judge an old, young, sick, or otherwise weakened animal and single it out for attack. Strong, healthy adults of many potential prey species can be dangerous.

The corroboration dogs most prefer is scent. A dog can be virtually "blinded" by a subject that is motionless when the wind is from the wrong quarter. If their fallback sense, sound, is not serving them well at the moment, they may have to fall back even a notch further and try taste. That can be unfortunate.

Bears, or ursids, shared a common ancestor with the canids about 60 million years ago. Miacis was his name. They still share common traits and the inability to identify a standing figure without benefit of smell is one of them. I have stood and watched kodiak bear, Alaskan Peninsula brown bear, North American black bear, Asian black bear, and polar bear all act bewildered because they knew *something* was there but they didn't have the wind coming to them from me. It is often the same with dogs except that bears, despite their size, tend to be cautious, which is a good thing for the naturalist in the field. Bears snuffle and *woof,* or they chop their jaws when they can't determine a presence. The latter sound is less than reassuring to the observer afoot. It can prelude an unfortunate encounter of the worst kind. Dogs and even wolves are generally much less cautious. Most dogs, conditioned to be brazen by their

life at our side, will go up and investigate. At the very
least they will bark in frustration if they are getting too
few signals to make a determination.

Years ago in Alberta I was following a pack of wolves
on foot. Actually we were playing a game of visual tag in
some relatively open woods. I just couldn't get a good
look at them. They weren't really very worried about me
or they would have simply vanished, but they weren't
being cooperative either. They just kept moving ahead of
me and from time to time I would get a fleeting look at a
tail and rump. It was near the end of December and the
Arctic was sending down some staggeringly cold air. I
stood it as long as I could. At last, since my camera was
frozen anyway, I started the long trek back to the field
south of the woods where my truck was parked.

Despite the fact that I was wearing a heavy scarf and the
hood of my parka was pulled up and tied tightly around
my face in a vain attempt not to become an ice statue, I
could feel the hairs on my neck rise. Something beyond
my five senses told me I was not alone. I turned and there
was the pack of wolves, led by a leggy but very large and
heavy yellow and white wolf, trotting along right behind
me no more than two hundred feet away. When I turned
they stopped. Some of them sat down to study me and
decide exactly what or at least who I was. They could see
me, but they needed more information than that. In no
sense were they threatening, just naturally curious, as be-

Dog on a Boeotion amphora,
750 B.C.

fitted animals as intelligent as they were. I gave them the data they needed. I tend to talk to animals in just about all situations anyway, so it seemed very natural in that most interesting situation. Imagine, interacting with a pack of wolves in the frozen world of near Arctic Canada! After watching them for a minute or two, I called out. I didn't yell, but I did speak loudly:

"What the hell do you guys think you're doing?"

That was all the information they needed. They heard me. I was a human being and could not be trusted to observe any form of woodland etiquette. They took off instantly and dissolved the way wolves do into the sparse stand of trees behind them. Still frozen but wonderfully envigorated by having had a fine view of the pack, I resumed my trek. I never saw the wolves again. It was a singular privilege to have made their acquaintance. Many times since then I have regretted sending them back into their secret world so quickly. I should have spent more time just standing there as we watched each other and they waited for a scent or sound of confirmation. But it was far below zero and I come from a temperate race.

As for the rest of the eye structure, it is all pretty standard. Dogs do not surprise us in this quarter. Light is admitted to the eye through the cornea and focused on the retina by the lens. Between the cornea and the lens is an iris that is very light sensitive. Just as with our eyes, it dilates when the light is low in intensity to take in all of the visual data it can. The rods (rod-shaped cells) in the dog's retina outnumber ours, while we have more cones which are suited to defining detail in bright light. The dog's eye has a reflecting layer called the *tapetum lucidum* that intensifies light and gives the dog/wolf an advantage during its optimum hunting hours at dawn and dusk. That is known as crepuscular activity, as opposed to diurnal and nocturnal. A dog caught by the side of the road at night whose eyes "shine" is reflecting your headlights off its tapetum. It is not emitting original light any more than it is haunting the neighborhood, legends about dogs' eyes "burning bright" in the night to the contrary notwithstanding. Initially its irises will be wide open because it has been dark until your headlights intruded. The irises will contract, however, once they are struck by bright light and the dog will likely turn away. The beacons will fade and vanish. It will seem like lights going out. Some animals, deer for example, are often transfixed by lights and will stand staring at the source of disturbance until you pass. That facilitates "jacking," the illegal hunting or poaching of deer using a strong spotlight. Recently a sportsman intruding on our farm shot Lily, one of our incredibly gentle greyhounds, while jacking out of season. She was found on our back porch in a pool of blood. Our ever-accommodating veterinarian got out of bed, drove the extra mile, and Lily survived. I do so love the concept of capital punishment in selected cases.

All of the structures of the eye, and we have mentioned only a few of what are many, must be in proper relationship to each other or they are worthless. An eye significantly out of round couldn't gather light effectively and it certainly couldn't focus images. The whole world would become a blur. The dog's eye shape is maintained, as is ours, by clear, colorless fluids, the vitreous and aqueous humors, under precise pressures. It is a truly miraculous device, the eye, and dogs put theirs to good use. They do need that corroboration, however, much of the time.

I mentioned trajectory earlier. Let no one doubt the ability of dogs of the right breeds or mix to plot an angle of ascendancy and predict the angle of decay. Almost any dog can chase a ball, although true scent hounds, the ultimate being the bloodhound, may finally rely on their nose to make the final identification. Over the years too many Labrador and golden retrievers have joined our herd for us not to appreciate their incredible understanding of ballistic performance. Toss a Frisbee or throw a ball as high as you can into the sky and watch your retriever be in exactly the right spot when the missile comes down. Catching a ball time after time, day after day, can't be written off as luck. It represents the ability of dogs to not only follow a moving object, their best suit when it comes to vision, but to plot the arc it will describe and the point of impact when it returns to earth, as they instinctively know it must. If you want to be really mean, release a helium-filled balloon and watch your retriever try to figure that one out. They just can't believe their eyes.

Surely the highly refined, instantaneous computations involved in tracking trajectory and plotting impact aren't done consciously. They are reflexive, but reflexes have to come from some place and that someplace is the canine genetic package. Since no one, we assume, played Frisbee or *Get the Ball* with wolves, the singular art of trajectory prediction has to be something we have built in. We obviously made a good job of it. Try throwing a ball just once for a dog. It would be like eating only one peanut or potato chip. Try to ignore the importuning of a golden retriever who has brought you his tennis ball, the greatest

treasure he possesses. Possesses! It is the dog that is possessed and your arm that soon feels as if it is dislocated.

If you discover the get-the-ball imperative built into a random-bred dog you are almost certainly seeing a dog with some retriever genes built in; either that or terrier blood. Terriers were designed to follow motion with enormous precision. The rodents and other so-called vermin they were meant to pursue are fleet and evasive little critters.

Even very small, unlikely breeds, Yorkshire terriers, for example, can display an uncanny understanding of trajectory and site of impact, although a less likely hunting dog than the Yorkshire terrier is difficult to imagine. Yet witness the remarkable story of Ludo, a quite private story from a typical American home. Americana, if you will.

Some years ago, Ludo, named for Ludovic Kennedy, the British television newsman, ruled our home with his light-hearted charm, style, and grace. One evening at a dinner party my mother-in-law (who is also British, frightfully British I might say) turned an unfortunate bilious green. Her new color was unmistakably progressing to-

ward aquamarine when it became clear that something had
to be done, and with some dispatch. More dutiful than
homicidal, I sped to her aid and applied a classic demon-
stration of the Heimlich maneuver. Unfortunately I was
apparently unable to totally mask my darker side and did
crack a fragile rib or two which I do not believe was originally intended to be part of the therapy protocol. A piece
of roast beef shot out of Phyllis's mouth, having been
dislodged from her throat where it was quickly bringing
her long and industrious life to a close. Ludo, ever watchful
for unexpected food offerings, flew up and neatly snatched
the piece of beef out of the air before it could hit the floor.
My mother-in-law was ungrateful, complaining for weeks
about how I had tried to kill her, completely ignoring her
Technicolor display that had prompted my assault. Ludo
remained even more watchful after that, never losing his
faith in serendipity. All dogs are optimistic, perennially.

Are dogs color-blind as has so often been suggested?
Apparently not. We can't look through a dog's eyes and
know empirically what they see (any more than we can
with each other's eyes), but they have enough cones to
indicate that although they do not see their surroundings
as a riot of color they do enjoy a pastel world of sorts.
Their color perception is subtle, softer than our own, but
its real importance is not clear. Here again, though, nature
is not fond of wasted resources so there must be some
survival advantage. One tends to think, though, that a
color-blind wolf/dog would not be terribly handicapped
during its preferred hours of hunting activity, dusk and
dawn. Perhaps the amount of color dogs and wolves can
see marks a stage in evolution. Perhaps the wolf was en
route to higher visual experiences when we snatched our
dogs from its loins. Perhaps the dog will continue in the
same direction.

One factor in visual observation: dogs tend to accept
things as they are. They do not worry about a great many
minor details unless some other sense confirms the pres-

ence of significant new data and signals them to pay attention. Cats, I think, tend to worry more about visual trivia than most dogs do. An example:

During Christmas week, 1990, a bitter cold time as I recall, a litter of random-bred puppies of the general German shepherd type was born in northern Baltimore County, Maryland. One of those puppies had five legs, two of them emanating at rakish and thoroughly useless angles off the right shoulder. In every other respect the puppy has proven to be normal.

The owner of the dam was apparently less than a perfect humanitarian and took the oddly constructed puppy out and left it in a snowbank to die. It couldn't have been much more than a week old. By some miracle an unknown person of higher moral fiber found the puppy and although we can't identify that person we acknowledge them here with thanks and a salute. The puppy, near death, was turned over to a volunteer humane group who frantically set to work to keep the puppy alive. Eventually it ended up with Dr. Alan Frank, our veterinarian. Reckoning that the two misshapen legs would be a hindrance and of no help, he operated and at six weeks of age, give or take a day or two, the five-legged puppy became a three-legged puppy with somewhat brighter prospects. My daughter, Pamela, and her eldest daughter, Sarah, did what they have been genetically predisposed to do. When they heard about the puppy they went to the hospital to adopt it and bring to an end its abuse and times of woe and sorrow.

When there are small children around to claim the prerogative of naming new pets, animals can get some very strange names. However, deciding how a pet shall be known for all of its life is an important step in the initial bonding of child and animal and so helps pets help children. Pets enable children to bridge out of their selfish little worlds and care for and about something beyond their own egocentric needs or wants. That is just one of the things pets do for small people. (We have a short-haired cat that

came to us as a waif, one of many we have in fact, that
Sarah, at five, named Fluffy Louise. She is about as *fluffy*
as I am. But how important is that?)

At any rate, at five-and-a-half, Sarah on the way home
from the hospital with her new three-legged puppy pon-
dered the little animal and the vibes she was getting, and
settled on Chloe Sweetpea as the appropriate expression
of the experience. (Is that any worse than Tripod, which
is probably what you or I would have named her?) My
son-in-law, Joe, was heard to murmur, however, that
some day he hopes they can get a dog he can call Thor.
As for the bonding? I was away shooting a television seg-
ment in Latin America for "20/20" when Sarah told me
about the new adventure on the phone.

She said: "Granddad, I know she is handicapped, but in
my heart she is perfect."

To the point of dogs and the visual experience: Chloe
Sweetpea went home to a house full of cats as well as Zack,
the yellow Labrador retriever who wags his tail even when
he is asleep, Annie, the Jack Russell terrier who has the
heart of a *Tyrannosaurus rex* when she suspects there is a
rat in the barn, and Luke, the golden greyhound with the
eyes of a deer, so beautiful, totally wasted on a male dog.

All of the cats and dogs instantly hated Chloe Sweetpea,
recognizing at once a bad idea when they saw one. Sleep
is impossible with a sprite around that attacks without
warning, trying to amputate by brute force everybody's
tails and ears. She barks and bites the other animals as the
tyrant all puppies are, and since she never had four legs,
even at an intermediary stage, she charges around like a
wonky E.T., giving neither quarter nor peace. The cats
escape because they can go high, from whence they glower
down on the terror of the turf. The dogs, generally earth-
bound, can only get away by going outside and standing
around freezing. In time Chloe Sweetpea will learn her
manners and somehow, I suspect, the other animals know
in their hearts peace will return. So far there has been no

significant counterattack, but the suffering within the pack is pitiful to see.

The point is the other dogs apparently haven't noticed that the puppy is different. Dogs can't count—I believe that can be safely said—so the actual difference between three and four is undoubtedly well beyond their reach. Still, Chloe Sweetpea is different. She is built differently from any dog they have ever known. She moves differently, certainly, but the other dogs in her household have not shown any curiosity about those facts. All they see is not the trivia of her construction but the undeniable fact that the new kid on the block is a first-class pain in the pinnae and caudal appendage.

4

THE MOST astounding conventional sense a dog has (one that we can presently acknowledge as a sense without being considered a bit spooky) is the sense of smell. A dog's nose is truly a many-splendored thing.

In 1982, dog trainer Milo D. Pearsall and veterinarian Dr. Hugo Verbruggen published a book on the subject of the dog's sense of smell called *Scent* (Alpine Publications, Loveland, Colorado). It contains a very good nasal analogy. A constituent chemical in human perspiration is butyric acid. If a single gram, a small drop, of that chemical were released in a ten-story building and it evaporated and spread uniformly throughout the structure, we might be able to pick it up by sniffing at a window, but only at the moment of or very shortly after release. (Gives you more respect for deodorants, doesn't it?)

But a dog! If the same chemical in the same quantity were spread over a city the size of Philadelphia (there has to be a lot of butyric acid in Philadelphia already, but fortunately it is not concentrated in anything as huge as drops), a dog could pick up on it anywhere within the city limits up to an altitude of three hundred feet.

Is that precisely, demonstrably, absolutely, exactly true? Who knows or cares? It makes the point. Empirically it can be shown that dogs can pick up on some odors in

concentrations of one part per trillion. And that is nothing to sniff at. That is, in fact, exactly, absolutely amazing.

Parenthetically, as we consider the dog's sense of smell, ask yourself how a dog stands living with us. Forget butyric acid. What about a roast leg of lamb when we deny our dog a place at the table? What must an air refreshener spray be like, hair spritz, insecticides in aerosol form, ammonia in floor and window cleaners? We must create a world of temptation and a cosmos of discomfort. We are a stinky lot and when we aren't being very, very good we are just awful.

One thing is certain, if we had even ten percent of a dog's sense of smell we would have a totally different chemical agenda for the world we inhabit. We might be amazed by the number of things now essential to our way of life that would be not only no longer essential but downright intolerable. We almost never take the dog's nose into account, however much we profess to love our pets. They are truly long-suffering, or perhaps sniffering.

Human beings beset by a sudden onset of small sensations may be transfixed by them, but that is usually only for a very short period of time. Recall what an indoor

Pack of hounds, from "The Sportsman's Repository," 1820.

swimming pool smells like, a locker room, a laundry, a greenhouse or flower shop, a butcher shop, a woodworking shop, an automobile repair facility, or a kitchen when garlic is in use. We recognize them when we first encounter them, but unless a smell is overwhelmingly awful and brings us near to a point of nausea we are unlikely to linger long on the sensation. It goes away as we suffer a kind of nose fatigue. In a sense we deny it. We are fortunate, in fact, that filters kick in for us on each of our five recognized sensory reception channels. If we didn't filter, I should think the world would be just about impossible for us to bear.

Dogs, apparently, don't do that, at least not with the sense of smell. A bloodhound of record once followed a scent trail that stretched one hundred and fourteen miles. It had, almost needless to say, a relay of handlers. It could never have made that remarkable run if its nose had been easily bored and quit on it. Scent is so important to the dog/wolf's way of life that it is not readily turned off or ignored. It is always there, right out in front, coaxing the animal on. In every imaginable sense of the expression dogs follow their noses.

The nasal cavity of the dog starts at the nostrils or external nares and runs all the way back to the rear edge of the animal's palate. The area of the cavity where the smell-sensing ethmoidal cells are located can contain one and a half cubic inches of air in man, on average, but four times that in a German shepherd—a full six cubic inches.

Just as in man, the dog's nose is divided into two channels divided by a septum made of cartilage. The flow of air is directed by a series of thin bony scrolls known as turbinates in the two channels. These turbinates greatly increase the surface area within the nose. When a dog is breathing naturally the current of air remains pretty well below the more sensitive areas and is directed on a downward path toward the trachea and thence to the lungs. If particles of special interest to the dog come in with the

"Villager with Pack of Dogs," seventeenth-century Dutch, by Dirck Stoop, shows a greyhound lean from training in hunting.

normal air flow, the dog will react by sniffing, creating eddies and currents that roll the air upward across the ethmoidal cells.

It should be stressed that the dog's nose, like its ears and eyes, provides a means of collecting information for the brain to deal with. It is the brain that smells, sees, and hears, in the sense that it evaluates incoming data and tells the animal what if anything to do in response. Much more of the dog's brain is given over to the interpretation of scent information than is the case with our brain. That, again, suggests just how sensitive a dog's sense of smell is. The two sides of a dog's nose are equally equipped to detect scent particles. The brain, by judging what each side of the nose is telling it, can direct the dog to the source of the smell. The exchange, the turnaround time, in a situation where a dog needs that direction from central control is virtually instantaneous. The computer on which I am making these observations is slower than a dog's brain. If you put a hot jalapeño in your mouth you will not be aware of a time-lapse as information goes up for evaluation and comes back down as instructions to spit it out. It will all happen instantaneously, or at about the speed of electric current traveling along a wire. So it is with the dog.

From passively receiving vague scent signals the dog changes to a mode of actively pursuing them. It is the pursuit of chemical knowledge and it excites a dog as almost nothing else does. The trick in feeding a sick or finicky dog is to increase the olfactory excitement level of the food you want it to eat. A little garlic, liver, kidneys, cheese, gravy, leftover soup of many kinds, bacon grease, pan drippings—all of those things and many others can get a dog to eat. It is very hard for a dog to turn its nose up at anything that smells good.

As for the term excitement applied to odor, read on if you are not eating. Skip ahead to the place marked **#@*#** if you are finicky.

Years ago a photographer came to do a magazine layout of me with our family animals. She seemed a nice enough sort, but she came from a place in Europe (I dare not be any more culturally insensitive than that, I dare not) where personal hygiene is apparently not regarded as a top-of-the-card item on everyone's agenda. It was a blistering hot day and we were all manufacturing butyric acid like crazy, but she was something else. She operated on a higher olfactory plane. She wore a tank-top dress that may once have been cleaned, but you would never have known it. Black hairs, rather long ones in fact, showed from her armpits glistening with perspiration. They seemed glued to her skin. She was in condition red and one really did want to get upwind of her. The cloud of self that hung about her approached the pathological.

The first beasts asked to pose with me were bloodhounds: Yankee, the splendid champion (who has been the subject of a book on his own) and his daughter, Penny. Normally they were very well-mannered dogs but clearly we were not living in normal times. In fact, the two of them acted as if they had died and gone to bloodhound heaven. Every gene they had inherited fairly throbbed for expression and realization. Their two-thousand-five-hundred-year history kicked in like a giant engine. They were bewitched.

As I sat holding Yankee, trying to look as if everything was as it should be in heaven and on earth, Penny gave the lady with the Leica the most ferocious goose. She reacted appropriately with a pelvis forward quickstep and as I tried to retrieve Penny good old Yankee gave her an inquiring nose-poke up front that just about doubled her over. It was a social occasion from hell. It was an impossible situation for any of us to have been in. My guest was just too ripe for bloodhounds to ignore. They bore in on her at every opportunity trying to check out particularly rich deposits. It was as if someone had inadvertently left a block of Limburger cheese on the kitchen counter overnight, a *warm* overnight.

Trying to keep the two giant hounds' minds on business was out of the question. They were onto something big and they knew it. Every time she moved they followed her with their noses while I struggled to keep them from making closer inspection sorties. I finally gave up on the bloodhounds; it was just too much to ask of them. We tried Lizzie, a basset hound, known to all as a perfect lady. Brought to the posing zone by my wife who was as red in the face as I was, Lizzie took one sniff and began barking and howling what I assumed to be her congratulations. We finally gave up photography and had iced tea—in the garden. There is no doubt about it, odors can excite dogs.

#@*#The dog's nose is a complex structure and is the only part of the dog's body where actual sensory tissue is directly exposed to the real world outside of the animal. That tissue consists of three different kinds of cells, one of which is the olfactory cell or sensory receptor. Those sensitive cells have very small hairlike structures, or cilia, that protrude from the membrane and are bathed in mucus.

A seventeenth-century Flemish painting by Adriaen Brouwer shows a woman de-fleaing a dog.

The mucus apparently picks up the chemical particles that constitute "smell," transmit the particles to the cilia and they, in turn, send along the information they have gathered to the cell proper. The number of cilia a sensory nerve has working for it in the outside world appears to correlate with just how sensitive that animal is to odors. Pearsall and Verbruggen give a sample cilia-per-cell count:

Frog	6–12
Rabbit	9–16
Rat	15–20
Cat	40
Human being	6–8
Dog	100–150

Clearly, the dog has a very serious nose. An additional set of comparative statistics: the actual number of olfactory cells that all those cilia swimming in mucus report to is of the utmost importance in rating noses. We have about five million such cells working for us while the dog has anywhere from one hundred and twenty-five to two hundred and twenty million. Is it any wonder that the bloodhounds that probably have the most keenly developed nose of all dogs went off the deep end over the lady photographer? If I could smell her well enough to find her objectionable with my pitiful nose, imagine what the bloodhounds were experiencing.

Not exactly parts of the sense of smell but parts of the nose complex are the sinuses. They serve a number of functions. One of them is providing resonance chambers for dogs when they communicate with their own kind, or with us. Whining or even barking would sound very different without that sound-enhancing nasal cavity and the sinuses that run off from it like separate echo-filled rooms.

Dogs, like many other animals including species as diverse as cats, rattlesnakes, and big-horn sheep, have an extra organ in the nasal cavity. It is the vomero-nasal area or Jacobson's organ. There is the hint that we once had

one, too, but that is ancient history, literally. Animals equipped with the organ can taste the air. But that is all beyond our understanding. We can't experience it and can only acknowledge it intellectually. In the desperation born of ignorance we keep trying to shove it all together as smell. It isn't. Tasting air is apparently a real experience for those having the equipment. It is an alternate form of chemoreception.

Even human beings can probably detect up to four thousand different smells. No one knows how many dogs can distinguish with the incredible apparatus they have. It is entirely possible that the number is smaller, more intense, certainly, but over a shorter, more germane spectrum. Dogs do not seem to be turned on by the smells that arouse the artist in each of us. Attar of roses is a thumping *so-what?* to a dog, while a nice big pile of manure, the parings from a horse's hoof, Lincoln logs from a cat box, or a dead skunk by the road—now *that* is smelling the way it is meant to be, so say our dogs. The dog's sense of smell is purely functional and not an aesthetic pursuit. Survival is what it is all about there on the primeval level. Species survival by the production of a suitable number of pups, individual survival by the acquisition of food, sex- and food-oriented smells are what is important, and that is understandable.

I am not sure why dogs roll on dead skunks and fresh manure, but they do it. Any number of explanations are encountered. Some scholars say it is to mask their own odor so that when they hunt they won't be detected by the prey they seek. Maybe. But then, dogs that have really worked up a good stinky fur are terribly interesting to other dogs. Could this be communication, one dog telling the other members of its pack that they have come upon animals that smell *like this,* or at least generate material that smells this way? Could it be an invitation to the hunt? It has also been suggested that it is like a male dog urinating where other male dogs have done the same thing. That would be staking claims. That doesn't seem right, though. I don't think a dog can generate an odor that would overwhelm fresh manure or a road-killed skunk. Still, we really know nothing of what it is like to deal with odors on a virtually ethereal plane. Maybe dogs smell more than dead skunks do, to other dogs. (If your dog does roll on a skunk or otherwise acquires that woodsy smell, take him outside and wash him with tomato juice, lots and lots of tomato juice, then in warm water using yellow laundry soap. It will work until he gets wet, then the smell will come back. Either way, burn your clothes. You may want to know that that will be necessary before taking on the project. Oh, yes, and shower, outside if possible. Expect inquiring looks for a few days.)

The bottom line? No one knows why dogs do such seemingly antisocial things. Apparently it is not antisocial among their own kind. I have a suggestion. Maybe they do it for no good reason whatsoever. It could be a vestige of their lives as wolves. It is likely that some of the things that dogs do are instincts gone somewhat wrong because of the process of domestication. That is as likely to be a valid explanation as the others, I think.

Then there is the matter of pheromones. Many, perhaps all animals produce odors that are territory markers, warnings, or sex attractants within their own species. Deer have

seven different glands that produce communicating odors.
Fruit bats produce them to deposit on tree limbs to establish
their roosting or hanging spot. As mentioned above, male
dogs produce it in their urine. Cats do, too. Some animals,
some moths, for example, use smell the way bats and
porpoises use hearing, at levels we can't even imagine.
Those huge "antennae" on some moths' heads are not
sound receivers at all, but scent receptors. A male moth,
it is said, can detect a female moth's sexually inviting pher-
omone at a distance of a mile. What is a fragment of a drop
of fragrance dispersed in the air for a distance of a mile in
parts-per-trillion or skillion or more? It is simply beyond
our ken, but we know that odor is a legitimate, functioning
form of communication. Can it be orchestrated differently
by different animals? We don't know if there is a creative
way to lay odors on top of odors and if it can be an individual's accomplishment. That is way out there, far out
of our reach. But dogs know and they play their game
every day. If there are scent symphonies, odor concerti,
smell poems, we just may never know. It is nice, somehow, to think that dogs have this for themselves, and other
animals of course. We are excluded. It is not ever to be a
part of our experience. When we can hear like a porpoise
and smell like a moth or even a dog we will probably have
long since had to change our names. We won't be human
beings any more. It makes animals more interesting, I
think. The inexplicable really isn't, unless, like us, you are
the product of stunted growth. Our noses are definitely
that.

A dog's nose is something for us to wonder at. It is
perfectly remarkable and reminds us that there is a world
out there that we can never know. At least not as human
beings.

5

TASTE AND SMELL are distinctly different senses in that they pass along discrete information on separate nerve channels to different receiving centers in the brain. Indeed, while taste and smell generally work together as chemical reception modes, they can be viewed apart, up to a point. I don't think taste really amounts to all that much working alone. Think of eating with a stuffy nose. Without vapors arising from the back of the mouth up into the nose, the experience is pretty uninspiring—unless, of course, you are eating Indonesian food or lay the wasabi a little thick on your sushi. And we must remember that Jacobson's organ is also in there working to break out chemical information for analysis in the case of dogs.

When a dog approaches a substance, be it half covered with leaves on the forest floor or in his own dish on the kitchen floor, he has a whole array of devices on hand for analysis and interpretation. And he has the brain to sort it out and consider all the evidence before drawing any conclusions. It is a very neatly integrated system designed to help the animal as dog or wolf survive one of the most time- and energy-consuming tasks he must undertake during his lifetime—food-getting. Doing it right means survival. Doing it wrong in an amazingly complex world of chemicals can mean death. We can lose sight of the fact

that a banana split in front of us on a soda fountain counter
is nothing more than a heaped and decorated pile of chemicals. I suppose, in a sense, we are, too. It is chemicals a
taste system must deal with.

Touch is a part of the process. Touch supplies the brain
with information on texture, smell gives central control
preliminary information from floating particles sucked free
and available to the animal's nose, and taste buds undertake
a chemical breakdown of the material for yet more precise
data. Add the input from Jacobson's organ and you have
a pretty awesome set of interpretive devices working in
concert.

When a dog takes something into its mouth, saliva carries particles or dissolved fragments of the material to taste
buds where chemical analysis is undertaken without conscious direction. As with us, it is automatic. It is unusual
for a dog to actually take something into its mouth (except
when it is chewing nice stinky things like bedroom slippers
and chicken bones) unless it really is going to process it as
food, i.e., swallow it. He is generally warned off bad-news
food before going that far. That does not always work
with puppies.

The back of the tongue is more richly endowed with
taste buds than the front or the sides. Thousands of nerve
cells feel out the chemicals being analyzed and send the
data up and back. The return, again, is instantaneous and
the dog knows what it is dealing with and reacts accord-
ingly. The substance is dropped or crunched and swal-
lowed and the outside source pursued, avoided, or ignored.
It is all designed so the animal can survive and feed another
day, during which time it just may reproduce, installing
the system in another generation of its kind.

Generally dogs prefer to avoid very hot tastes—jalapeño
peppers, for example—and very cold ones like alcohol and
peppermint. The taste buds can easily identify these categories because they break tastes down into five basic modalities; sweet, sour, salt, bitter, and water. Working alone

or in concert, those five cover everything the dog can take into its mouth. They are to taste what primary colors are to vision.

The dog's brain has a large store of information about taste that came to it as part of its genetic package. It is usually not necessary for a dog to have had earlier experience with a taste for it to react appropriately. Dogs can learn, however, i.e., add to their store of specific taste information. We are not sure how the scan is done, but by using the combination of the five taste modalities from the nerve clusters servicing the taste buds, plus texture, smell, and the Jacobson's input, the brain can make a determination very, very quickly. In fact, the decision is made and the command dispatched well before the dog can begin to swallow. That, of course, is essential to avoid deadly mistakes. Dogs that gulp food, however, can get into deep trouble. A dog of ours, a bloodhound, in a moment of wild abandon and good fun, snapped a bumblebee out of the air. The angry little beast didn't remain imprisoned for long, only long enough to respond to the insult. The poor puppy didn't understand what had happened. He did, however, leave future low-flying bumblebees alone. Not exactly taste, of course, but an illustration of a lesson learned. The trouble with chemical mistakes is that an animal can die learning that oven cleaner is bad stuff.

A display of the brain's awesome interpretive and decision-making power can be witnessed whenever an inexperienced dog first encounters a toad. Toads, like most amphibians, have poison-secreting glands on their shoulders just behind their tympanic membranes, on their thighs, and often on their legs. In some species their backs have clusters, too. Some species have more of these glands than others and in some amphibians the poison is really deadly. Frogs in South America (the arrow-poison frogs) and some in Australia (the catholic frogs, with a small *c*) are true killers. Even some of our domestic salamanders, efts, and newts can do a terrible job on a cat or dog that

"English Water Spaniel," 1769, by George Stubbs, is of a breed that no longer exists.

actually eats one, or even mouths a specimen for too long.

Generally, though, dogs don't eat amphibians. Those clusters of poison glands do just what they were designed to do—they protect the little animals. Even snakes spit them out. Birds have virtually no tasting ability. Some, like the herons, do eat every amphibian they can find. They survive what a dog could not.

A very jolly toad lives somewhere near the door to my study during the spring, summer, and fall months. I have to be careful not to step on him because he apparently has blind faith in his immortality. I have taken to carrying a flashlight so when I quit work at night and head for the house I won't annihilate the trusting little soul with my heel.

One day a bloodhound puppy was exploring the garden near my door to see what kind of trouble he could get into. He spied the toad and like all puppies reacted by taking it into his mouth. The turnaround time was less than a second. The unharmed but I am certain indignant toad lay upside down amid the marigolds trying to figure out what that had been all about and the puppy was heading away, probably doing pretty much the same thing. It wasn't until an hour had passed that Sweet William stopped looking at me sideways as if it had been my fault. After all, he was new on earth and as trusting as the toad. Apparently I should have warned him. I couldn't explain that if he stopped trying to stuff the whole world into his already cavernous maw, I would have time to guide him. Puppies do seem to want to inhale the whole world. Perhaps that is because they are teething, perhaps it is just childish exploration, or perhaps it is their way of building on their store of taste data. All puppies do it.

The toad is an object lesson of sorts. Although I have never tasted one, I am certain that they are bitter, and bitter is the taste of most naturally occurring toxins dogs must avoid if they are to grow up and reproduce. Nature has

been all-wise in this matter. She has made most of her poisons in a red-alert modality and made most animals so that they are repelled by that taste category. Of course, we have come along and created deadly poisons like antifreeze and made them sweet and tempting to dogs and children.

What tastes do dogs like? Although dogs are truly individualists, there are certain tastes that have virtually universal appeal. When you see handlers at a dog show holding their charges' attention by holding something out and up, baiting, that bait is almost always liver. Beef liver slabs are baked in the oven on cookie sheets and then broken into chips about an inch square. Dogs love liver, kidneys, and the other animal material the British refer to as *offal*.

Most dogs love scrambled eggs, animal fats such as butter, cheese and bacon, ham, beef and lamb, fowl; and many dogs like fish very much, too. Although they don't need it, once they have been weaned, most dogs like milk. And though it isn't good for them, dogs generally enjoy chocolate. In fact, sweetness is an enticing taste modality for just about all dogs. Unfortunately, sugars do to dogs just what they do to people—they make them fat. And dogs can suffer from diabetes; a great many, in fact, do. Dogs love crunchy textured things if taste and smell do not warn them off. Dogs love peanut butter but hate it when the sweet goop sticks to the roofs of their mouth. Dogs are attracted by starches like mashed potatoes but prefer it even more if there is a bit of gravy on it. To a point, dogs like things that are salty. But after that, it is pretty much each dog for itself.

Bozo was a Boston terrier that adored tomatoes despite their acidic quality. That is not all that unusual. Jedidiah the bloodhound did, too. Coyotes and foxes raid melon patches and many of them eat wild berries. We had a golden retriever named Jeremy that was fairly mad for watermelon and a random-bred airedale cum German shepherd kind of bitch named Nel Gwynn that loved corn on the cob. She would lie on the porch with a well-stripped cob in her mouth for hours, sucking and humming with pleasure. We had a dog that liked apples and one that would go through hoops for a bit of cucumber. Dogs do their own things, some more than others. I met a bloodhound once whose owner rewarded her with a dill pickle after a successful trail run. Most bloodhounds are rewarded with the ever-handy bits of baked liver. Not her! Give her a kosher dill pickle that would turn off just about any other dog in the world and she was one happy hound.

Some dogs develop taste preferences and don't like to deviate. They just don't trust new tastes. Others remain puppies all their lives. They want to gulp down everything in sight, moving or stationary. Duncan, our border collie, is picky and distrustful. He is like a cat. Until he is certain what you are offering him is something he knows and can trust he approaches your fingers slowly and carefully, never taking his eyes off your face. He acts as if you were trying to poison him. Zack, the Lab, on the other hand, will inhale your hand and forearm if you offer him roofing nails. He is completely trusting. I would rather he'd be suspicious.

Factors other than taste can affect the way dogs approach food. Lily, our very beautiful greyhound bitch, came to us with a wagonload of emotional baggage. We already had our first greyhound rescue, the wonderful Reggie, and reckoned we had room for a second. (The number has grown to three and we are actively considering a fourth.) These are greyhounds that have come off the race track. That brutal business (I just can't think of it as a sport; it is a spectacle) kills off about fifty thousand dogs a year. Once they stop winning, five percent of the canine athletes are selected for breeding, and the other ninety-five percent, still very young dogs, are killed. These are dogs that could live into their teens.

And so we went to see Betty Rosen, our local greyhound rescue lady. There is a network of these saints around the

A seventeenth-century copy of Albrecht Dürer's "St. Hubert." The saint changed from an avid huntsman to a protector of animals.

country. She had two bitches available. Gretchen, a black-and-white girl, boldly marked, was all over us. She had the world on a string. She trusted anything on two legs. Lily cowered. She was an exquisitely dainty brindled bitch to which something bad had apparently happened. She was

Taking dogs to field trials, 1907.

more than shy, she was truly frightened, especially of me. She would remain cautious of men for the months it took us to turn her around. We did decide to take the sad Lily over the gregarious yahoo called Gretchen because it was obvious that the latter could make it anywhere. She had the world on the half shell and she knew it. Lily was the kind of dog that often gets passed around until she is so insecure and crazy she ends up being put to sleep. We were sure she had potential, but she did need some experienced hands to help her and guide her.

Lily turned the corner in about six months. She is friendly, even gregarious, and she allows people to have bass voices. She turned out just fine. The last vestige of her emotional scars centered on dog biscuits. We use a reward system at our place that allows us to let our dogs run as free as they love to be. Coursers like greyhounds can really make use of a thirty-five-acre backyard. And it is very good for the other dogs that try to keep up with

them. It is wonderful exercise. But dogs have to be re-
callable. They all know when they hear the call it means
"cookies" are waiting, and they come in through the back-
door like an avalanche and form an eager and expectant
semicircle around whichever one of us is doing the cookie
honors. It is a very exciting time and a great opportunity
to interact with the dogs.

Each dog gets his cookie and grinds it up as fast as he
can before pushing in for another. For the longest time,
not Lily. Her nose was there waiting until she was actually
offered the treat. Then she backed up, shook, looked anxious, then bowed, stretching her front legs way out in front
with her rump in the air. She wanted her cookie as much
as the other dogs did, but she couldn't overcome some old
fear, something she had learned, and take it from your
fingers. Her cookie had to be tossed on the floor where
she grabbed it before the other dogs moved on it. This
went on for months, long after her other fears had been
mastered.

Finally we went for this last vestige of what had obviously been an unhappy childhood. We caught her by the
collar, opened her mouth with our fingers and put the
biscuit on her tongue. This wasn't necessary with any other
tidbits, just dog biscuits. She had obviously been baited
with biscuits, then hit. She wanted her biscuit, but she had
been conditioned to expect pain to come with it.

Needless to say, Lily has turned her last corner and trusts
the hand that feeds her biscuits, but her case does demonstrate that even a dog's desire for foods that it finds
highly palatable can be affected by conditioning.

A last observation about taste in dogs, i.e., the dogs'
taste, not ours. Puppies, after they are weaned, are best
put on a puppy growth food high in calcium and other
skeleton building minerals and nutrients. It is best to keep
them on it for a year, if possible. It is easier to keep them
happy with what is not the most terrific-tasting food in
the world as long as they do not know that that is not all

the world has to offer. (I tried some to see how bad it is.
It is bad. It is awful, in fact. I have tasted better things on
airplanes.) But it is hard to keep puppies down on the farm
once they have experienced Paree. Let a puppy taste a Big
Mac or a little bit of cheese and you have a potential food
brat on your hands. Taste, like odors, can turn a dog on
and it can turn him off.

6

THE LAST of the traditional senses we have to consider is touch. If we accept the input from Jacobson's organ as a full sense, and we really should, touch is number six.

Most dogs, you may have noticed, love this kind of input. They love to be touched. They find it reassuring. It does all kinds of things for them. It warns them of danger, it enables them to get comfortable, and it can be used in social bonding. It may also bring signals over surprising distances.

The tactile sense is always on duty and to some extent monitors conditions surrounding an animal on a moment-by-moment basis. Touch is akin to hearing and long ago, long before the first wolf howled or even before the first mammal emerged, they were one sense. Hearing broke away as a means of detecting vibrations in a fluid medium, air, while touch remained essentially an interpreter of hard data in close contact.

Hearing, then, is really touch of a special kind. It relies on rapidly repeated touches reaching the eardrum. Perhaps when Duncan, our border collie, "hears" our horses racing across a pasture he is touched on the pads of his feet as well as on his eardrums. Quantifying the role that touch plays in establishing distant phenomena as well as the animal's immediate environment is a little difficult to do.

A corded poodle, 1895.

Hair (fur, really) is an extension of the skin. When you touch a dog you cause individual hairs to bring pressure on the follicles imbedded in the skin. Nerves there accept the input and refer it to the brain for interpretation. (Try this on yourself: With the flat of your hand barely touch your own hair. It can be downright eerie if you concentrate on it and touch very lightly. If you are bald, work it out as best you can.) The brain instantly correlates the signals that have come from the nerves in the skin with what has been sent in from the ears, eyes and nose, and determines what if any reaction is required to keep the animal alive. That is what it is all about.

Certain kinds of touch, real temperature extremes, physically damaging blows, bites, kicks, scratches—those kinds of things register first as touch before they become broken bones and punctures. Sometimes, of course, an impact is so sudden and so overwhelming that it is academic whether that which cracks a leg bone was first a whisper of touch. The registration, analysis and reaction instructions are not that fast!

There are a number of different ways dogs like to be touched and they are usually easily interpreted as extensions of real life. Dogs, especially male dogs I think, like to have their chests scratched right between the front legs. They stand very still and get a silly, dazed look in their eyes. "I'll give you forty-eight hours to cut that out," they seem to be saying. When males mount or cover (a quaint euphemism) a female, their chests are on the female's spine. The inevitable pelvic thrust "scratches" the male's chest. When you scratch his chest, it is obviously terrific. Great associations. No reason not to do it. It can be a thing you share with your dog. Just play dumb and pretend you never read this paragraph.

Everyone knows that dogs like to be scratched behind the ears, each side equally. (If that is not so with your dog, have his ears checked by a veterinarian. There may be an irritation or infection there.) That is as raunchy as the chest-rub business. Courtship, foreplay if you will, includes ear nibbling and nuzzling in wolves and dogs. At least it should. Any dogs that do not observe these niceties are really *biff-bam* rough-and-tumble sorts. A well-mannered, nicely raised dog would certainly engage in a little gentle romancing before scratching his own chest.

Patting is the way we most frequently interact with our dogs physically. It is somehow reassuring to both man and dog and that is all to the good. Exactly what patting relates to or refers back to in the normal behavior of either species is not really clear. There are a number of theories, there always are, but it doesn't matter all that much. It could be a whole new thing we have invented. It could be a newly evolved dual tactile experience that dogs will refer back to if they ever become wolves again. Perhaps our theoretical dog-descended wolves will have to learn how to pat each other in order to successfully engage in social intercourse and maintain order.

Cuddling is a whole bunch of touch sensations and temperature sensations going on at the same time. No problem making a correlation there. A bitch "cuddles" her young to keep them warm and to stay in touch with them while she dozes. If one of them moves, she'll know it. It is a running inventory in a dangerous world. We also cuddle our young and a good snuggle/cuddle provides parent and child with some of the best quality time we have. Dogs like to cuddle with their masters, too. That is especially true when they are puppies. Some older dogs grow out of it, but, then, so do some kids. Whether it is kids or dogs, it is good time, valuable time, a time of special bonding. Heaven alone knows how many nerve endings are involved.

Some dogs live at the Plaza . . .

. . . and some do not.

It must be something like the number of stars in the Milky Way.

(I wish my wife wouldn't cuddle the large hounds in our bed. It is king-sized, I'll admit, but when a greyhound or a bloodhound shoots out its legs in a moment of special pleasure they are like spiked poles. Once a bloodhound that weighed one hundred and fifty pounds shot me right out of bed. My wife thought that was funny.)

Another big turn-on for dogs is the scratch and rub along the cheek, from the corner of the mouth back. Again, theories exist as to why this is such a sensitive area, but who really knows? I suspect that the dog, the ancestral wolf or some earlier ancestor, perhaps, has or had glands there used to deposit pheromones, scent signals, and that may relate to the same phenomenon in cats. It may be territorial. Cats and dogs, although very different animals

now, are both members of the Order Carnivora. At some
point they had common ancestors. Miacids are the likely
candidates. But that was between fifty and a hundred million years ago.

Touch-sensitive nerve endings on a dog's body are, of
course, extremely numerous. Each hair follicle is thus
equipped and there are others as well. The kinds on foot-
pads and the nose and lip areas are not tied to hairs. In
combination they all add up to a wonderful sense mech-
anism capable of providing a lot of information about the
world and giving a great deal of pleasure. We have witnessed the pleasure part in all of our dogs, each of which
has had its own little quirks and peculiarities.

Sense (that is pronounced *Sen-say,* but don't blame me,
he came with that name) is a blue merle Great Dane
roughly the size of a Belgian draft horse. The depth and
meaning of touch is clear with this great dog because he
is epileptic and has ferocious grand mal seizures. He is not
ferocious, but his terrible fits are. He lives with a friend
of ours now because we do travel a lot and he needs a
home where someone will be home every night who can
cope. Grace Froelich is one of those saintlike people who
can and will cope with anything that happens to any animal
anywhere.

While we had Sense here he would be found once every
seven to ten days on his side, paddling his legs and frothing
at the mouth. There is not much you can do for a dog
when he is really out of it, but by some instinct I felt I
should sit on the floor with him and pat him. At some
point he would get back in touch with reality and whenever
that happened he would be reassured by gentle physical
contact. I would be there waiting for him. At least that
was my theory. I don't know for certain that that was the
right thing to do, but I do believe it was. At least it gave
me something seemingly constructive to do in times of
stress. Tactile sensation is a two-way street. For dog lovers
dog patting feels right and good.

"The Start of the Hunt," the first of the Unicorn Tapestries. French, fifteenth–sixteenth centuries.

When a dog stands, there is a thin web of skin from the leading edge of the upper hind leg to the dog's body. When puppies act up, bitches sometimes nibble that web gently. Try it with your dog. Don't nibble it, for heaven's sake, but roll it between your thumb and forefinger. If you think your dog looks silly when you scratch his chest, try this one. They usually get a perfectly idiotic look on their faces. It takes them back to their childhood apparently, and it does actually settle them down. All of our dogs have been suckers for that one.

To make the greatest possible contact with our dogs I combine touch and sound. I make what I am sure are idiotic sounds using goofy voices while I give them a good scratch and rub. They love it. They wiggle, and push in for more. It is a pretty good idea to be away from other people when you do it unless you want people talking and pointing. Once you allow yourself to get into this kind of thing you can really sound pretty stupid. I've already mentioned dog biscuits, big news in our house. Try this: *"Hey, you guys, I think it is time to cookiate."* They go wild when I say that. They love it. Duncan loves it when I insult him, while I am scratching him. *"You are nothing but a dog, just a dog, and I shouldn't be wasting my time on you."* His eyes get absolutely glassy when I say that, particularly when I sound like a poor imitation of Mel Blanc. A combination of weird voices you wouldn't be caught dead using in public, along with food treats and a roster of tested rubbing zones, can bond you and your dog in a way that is truly special. Remember, while you rub, your dog is listening.

7

WE HAVE covered the five basic senses, the conventionally acknowledged ones, and one that is less conventional only because we don't have it and can only relate to it through our imagination. That is air-tasting, of course—the Jacobson's organ. So much for solid ground. We have inevitably come to that place in our time together where we have to risk walking on thin ice.

What makes the ice thin here? Lack of universal acceptance by accredited scientific bodies in the appropriate disciplines of the premises it is necessary for us to put forth for consideration here. (That is the kind of sentence accredited scientific bodies feel comfortable with.)

If you are a scientist you want to be absolutely certain that something exists before you go public with it. Not only that, you want to be equally well-informed on the subjects of why it exists, where it exists, how, for how long, when, and so what. Failing the ability to answer these questions and a good many more besides, you can reasonably expect to be skinned alive by your peers. Scientists seem to like nothing better than having at each other.

What you have, then, are scientists who, in general, have to live in deadly fear of their fellow investigators. In the final analysis, that is a good thing. It keeps scientists honest, it keeps them on a truly scientific path. Peer pressure enables us to have a measure of trust in what science tells us. What they tell us is almost certainly the truth *as it is understood at the moment*. It does not necessarily follow that it will always be true. By no means does it mean that. Far, far from it.

Truth does not stand still, no matter how much sense it seems to make at the moment. Truth is a dynamic, developing system of facts. But it inches forward, seldom does it leap. (Occasionally, though, it does. In the 1950s the Astronomer-Royal of Great Britain said something to the effect that all of the talk going around about astronautics was *poppycock*. Poor dear. How would you like to have lived through the sixties and seventies with that emblazoned on your forehead?)

Ultimately, although it may seem agonizingly slow to

The first greyhound race after a mechanical hare, at the Welsh Harp, Hendon, 1876.

the rest of the world, that is the way progress is made. We know of no other way. You would not want to send your son or daughter up in a spacecraft or undergo surgery yourself if the science involved had popped out of someone's imagination full-blown and flowering. That which slowly evolved from very hard, painstaking work is the science we can go on with confidence and upon which future science can be built.

A complaint often heard about the scientific method is the seemingly endless repetition of an experiment or test. That is essential to the process. If you make something happen in a laboratory and have properly recorded not only the results but the protocol, the precise steps you took to get those results, another scientist following the same protocol under the same conditions should be able to arrive at the same results. That endless repetition is what turns theories into scientific fact. By the same logical process, if you observe behavior in an animal, it should be able to be observed by other observers of equal skill. If it can't be, it may be that you were mistaken in what you reported or perhaps you happened upon an aberration. The world is full of them.

Nevertheless, it is perfectly all right for us to explore on ahead and see what tomorrow's truth might be. Thinking about possibilities does not become a scientific crime unless you get carried away and start proclaiming what you have thought about as fact. Thinking about something does not make it true. So, just be careful, as you speculate, not to declare the apparent facts that are revealed to be proven. We will be careful here, reasonably. I am perfectly willing as we embark on this journey to what may be other planes to admit that we are speculating. We cannot weigh, mount, pickle or pin the things we will be talking about. But then, we don't have to. We live with our dogs and can observe them in the intimacy of our homes, in the bosoms of our families. And we aren't going to lose a grant from the Museum of Natural History to study the taxonomy of spotted skunks because we try to understand why our dogs behave the way they do. No need to get silly, but we can probe ahead. So many interesting things may very well be hiding there.

The context for this exercise is interesting. I am sitting here looking at two books from a shelf in my library crammed with such books. One is called *Thinking Animals* by Professor Paul Shepard. The other is *Animal Thinking* by Dr. Donald R. Griffin. Fifty years ago you would have been drawn and quartered by the scientific community for saying that animals think. That would have been akin to shouting @#$% in church. In the same suffocating environment a suggestion that man is not the only tool-using animal was mortal sin and the idea that animals have emotions was a worse sin yet.

In the last fifty years we have watched unthinking, non-language using, unfeeling, non-tool-using beasts become something quite different even in the minds of orthodox science. Let us suppose (we can do that if we want to) that that view is still evolving as we consider here how our dog friends plug into the world around us. How do they perceive reality, or better yet, what is reality to them? Or them to Hecuba?

Oomiac was a Siberian husky who came to us as a young but fully adult dog literally on the eve of her scheduled execution. We saw her in a shelter in Virginia on death row and we just couldn't allow anything that beautiful to be killed simply because no one would care for her. We didn't need another dog—far from it—but asked for necessary adoption papers between tightly clamped teeth, all the while shooting we-must-be-crazy looks at each other.

When the formalities were over, Oomiac was brought out to us by a teenaged boy who broke down and sobbed. He really loved Oomiac, whom he had been caring for, but his parents wouldn't let him bring her home. Nice people. He had been almost sleepless for a week, knowing the clock was ticking and time was closing in on his special

friend. When he did sleep he apparently had nightmares. I thought he was going to kiss our hands as we assured him that his girl was going to be cared for as long as she lived. And she was.

Oomiac had the face of an angel, but the heart of a prostitute. If you let her out on her own, it was farewell for only she knew how long. Even though we had a decent piece of land, she was gone whenever she was given the opportunity to split. The other dogs came in when they were called. But not Oomiac. She would come meandering back hours or very often days later. She was always in good condition and didn't seem to be hungry or thirsty, so we suspected that she had another home. Obviously she was as casual with her other family as she was with us. This can happen with a dog that has been denied early experience in bonding. They may be decorative, they may be unfailingly pleasant (Oomiac was both of those things), but they may not be biddable, as my Scots friends would say. Oomiac was not biddable, she was decidedly casual. And that meant long walks on a leash just before bed every night, no matter what the weather. At least it gave us time together and the air where we lived was salty and fresh.

One evening, it was about eleven o'clock, Oomie and I were walking on a country road that ran parallel to the salt water inlet on which our house was set. Hog Creek, it is called, although I don't know why. There are a lot of stories about the area, some dating back to the days when the Accabonic Indians came there for the scalloping and clamming, but none reveal the origin of that name. There it was, running along off to our right, woods off to the left (there are A-frames and ticky-tacky ranch-style summer homes there now, which is one of the reasons we eventually left) and the night was as black and quiet as that proverbial tomb. All of a sudden Oomiac froze. She stared straight ahead. She was almost leaning into something. I asked her what was wrong and she barely flicked an ear at the sound of her name, but she wouldn't budge. She was rigid. I tried to turn her away. She pulled until I relaxed the pressure on her leash and then she went right back into her locked position. I tried to get her to go forward. No way. I moved around in front of her. She tried to look

around me. I petted her. Her muscles were taut. Something
had her literally transfixed. It was as if I weren't there. She
was alone with something on a different plane, something
known only to her.

I tried to get with the event, to share the experience.
Obviously, it would have been fascinating. I strained for
the same signals she was getting. No luck. I could hear
nothing, see nothing, smell nothing, taste nothing, and
nothing was touching me except my own clothing, my
wrist watch and Oomiac's leash in my hand. It occurred
to me later that maybe my friend didn't see, hear, smell,
taste or feel anything either. And maybe it wasn't her
Jacobson's organ. Maybe the signals were on a different
plane altogether, or different planes.

Earlier in our walk a raccoon had crossed the road in
front of us. Oomiac thought that was mildly interesting,
as would befit her wolf ancestry, but nothing more than
that. We had passed a couple of dogs apparently more
reliable than Oomiac who were taking their own late-night
constitutionals. Some of them came out of their yards to
investigate us. Oomiac thought they were worth a sniff
or two, but nothing more intense than that. Along the way
we smelled a skunk and Oomie sniffed up a good noseful
of that pungent information. We heard a deer, apparently,
off in the woods. Oomie listened and sniffed for confirmation of that. It was transient data, all so-so in importance. She had experienced all of it before, many times, in
fact. None of these encounters produced the kind of reaction I was witnessing to the Unknown.

Finally, Oomiac relaxed a little and agreed to go back
down the road. She did pull to look back a couple of times,
but finally we did go home and she curled up in her usual
spot and dropped her head, presumably to dream about a
secret world to which she had entry but I did not. It was
a classic situation. As a member of the more intelligent
species I would forever be denied access to something
that was exciting, enchanting, electrifying, terrifying or

entrancing to her species. I could peer off into the night as hard as I wanted to. I could strain my ears, sniff, intellectualize, but in the end would be forced to the conclusion that a couch potato of a sled dog had access to the world outside my front door that would forever be denied me, however many college degrees I assembled. There were planes of perception that were open to her, but denied to me. And so it is with our dogs, I believe, and that is what we might profit from understanding.

What are these avenues of input, how is the seemingly arcane information received? Whatever the channels are it seems certain the data is processed by the brain. I don't think we are speaking here of anything that is either phenomenal or paranormal. I am sure it is simply a matter of our not yet understanding in any great depth how animals relate to their surroundings. We don't give them credit for the things they can do.

If we do not have an ability parallel with or in some way referable to the ability of other creatures, I think there is a natural tendency to deny that anyone or anything has it. Even scientists are human (yes, truly they are) and probably suffer from this shortcoming as much as we do. Some things, of course, cannot be denied because they can be measured, there is a quantity involved. But no ruler, no scale, no gauge can be used to explain Oomiac's secret conversation with the night. Let us try to understand what her skills acutally were, or at least might have been.

Dr. Desmond Morris is always interesting. He is a keen observer of the natural world and an equally skilled reporter. He has a scientist's credentials, but dares state in popular terms what he knows or at least what he believes. In his recent book *Dogwatching* he asks the question, "Do dogs have a sixth sense?" He says yes, at least a sixth, and adds the caveat, "They can all be explained by biological mechanisms, although it is true that we are only just beginning to understand some of them." I agree with that. Remember, nothing *phenomenal or paranormal*. If a dog displays sensory acuity far beyond our own it is because he has the physical equipment to do it, just as he has the equipment to run. That is true even if we cannot quite locate where that equipment is or how it might work. There is no need to worry about it, though. Ignorance is transient. In time we will understand.

Dr. Morris suggests that the earth's magnetic field may

have a great deal to do with migration, in birds, mammals, fish and a few insects. Perhaps each place on earth is like a fingerprint, unlike any other. In fact, a map of the magnetic fields that surround us looks not unlike an exploded diagram of a fingerprint with a distinctive pattern of whorls and loops that is apparently infinitely variable. I have long felt that this was so, that many animals, including dogs, can interpret and utilize this magnetic data. There have been experiments where animal navigation was impaired by magnets used for that purpose. I suggest, further, that what we are opening up here has many layers, many levels of truth, perhaps like hearing in a bat or porpoise, or eyesight in an eagle. I suspect that it does. We don't yet fully comprehend the initial premise. We don't know how or where an animal as familiar to us as the dog receives the information or how it is correlated with other input. We have not even begun to penetrate the surface. Yet, almost certainly, at least one other sense exists that might be as keen and as important as any of the conventional or presently acknowledged ones are.

Using the earth's magnetic fields is something we do, too. The difference is we have to use electronic gear to detect and interpret them. For years we have used airborne equipment to map these magnetic features. Both the Soviets and the Americans created magnetic maps of Antarctica for scientific study. We use the magnetic fields that surround us. They are real, they are not spooky or weird. Very simply, they exist and we have known that for a long time.

It is at least a fair question to ask, may not dogs use them, too? Dogs, Dr. Morris points out, apparently can predict earthquakes and thunderstorms. I am certain they can, but I think we should separate the two natural phenomena because it would seem likely that different reception modes are involved.

First, earthquakes. We don't know how some animals know when these giant events are coming, but it is gen-

A post dog in World War II.

erally acknowledged that they do. In China researchers
have been experimenting with a variety of animals for
earthquake prediction and they are apparently satisfied that
animals do have this ability. The trick seems to be to figure
out how to interpret what the animals are telling us. We
can worry about how they do it later.

In California, investigators have been working with
species as far apart in the animal kingdom as cockroaches

and ground squirrels in determining if there is a way to get animals to tell us in advance what they can detect is happening deep in the earth. Progress is apparently being made. The research has been funded, so apparently some people feel it holds promise of benefit.

We know that earthquakes don't just up and happen like a jar being suddenly dropped or knocked off a shelf by a careless hand. There is a period of buildup and it is what happens during that period and in the earliest stages of the slippage that makes dogs restive, sets them to howling, makes them whine, pace, and scratch at the door. There is a natural tendency to assume that they feel vibrations. But that is only an assumption. Perhaps vibrations are part of it. There may be sudden, quirky changes in the earth's comfortable magnetic fields dogs are familiar with. That would be disconcerting, certainly. There may be very high frequency sounds produced as gases escape through crevices we have not yet detected. Earthquakes and the phenomena that precede them may have odor. Or, possibly, earthquakes may register with dogs and other animals through means as unfamiliar to us as magnetic detection. We aren't ready to deal with this one yet and can only speculate. Scientists will find out, they will unravel how dogs do what we are reasonably certain they do. They just haven't done it yet. We can be sure, however, that when tectonic plates begin to slide deep, deep below the surface of the earth, your dog is listening and almost certainly doing something else as well.

Now, thunderstorms. A number of things happen, we know, when an area is about to experience an electrical storm. There is an increase in ozone caused by lightning, but that occurs after the storm is underway. Even we can smell ozone. (It smells a little like the indoor swimming pool at the YMCA.) That ability could almost certainly be explained by the dog's keen nose. But what about *before* the storm?

Duncan knows when a storm is coming. He gets very

nervous. He is obviously upset. He can't get comfortable, he can't sit still. He is insecure, perhaps frightened, and we know from experience to get him inside and keep him there. At least in the house he can't get hurt by running blindly across roads and highways. He is that uptight. He has to be protected from himself.

Why? How? Possibly barometric pressure. There is nothing arcane about that, nothing more unusual than a weather report. Your radio and television will tell you all about a "low-pressure system" moving in from West Virginia or Addis Ababa. They will even quantify it for you: "The barometric pressure is 31.4 inches of mercury and falling." How many times have you heard that?

I believe very firmly that we are affected by dropping air pressure. It seems to make us uneasy; it makes some of us cranky. I don't know how it works in us, nor do I know how it might work in dogs. Perhaps it is a function of hearing. Maybe it does happen in the ear. But there could be something else involved. And if falling air pressure is detected by the ear, does that necessarily mean that that automatically makes it a phase or aspect of hearing, or does the ear serve another sense? Darned if I know. I do know that if I stay in Mexico City or Quito (they are both at 10,000 feet) for more than a few days I undergo a change of personality. I begin to lose my legendary, normal saintlike patience very quickly. I become less of a pussycat. Even Nairobi and Denver (at 5,000 feet) get to me after three or four days. I am a sea-level animal. When I used to scuba dive I was less than distinguished at the game. I hated going below twenty feet. As I said, sea *level*.

We have, then, through empirical observation (our own or that reported by others so often it is impossible to ignore), raised the probable or perhaps just possible number of dog senses from six to nine. We have added the probabilities of magnetic field detection, barometric pressure sensitivity, and a who-knows-what earthquake detection mode. I think we should go for one or two more before taking stock.

It is an established fact that rattlesnakes, copperheads, and their kin, animals known collectively as pit vipers or members of the family Crotalidae, have heat detectors in their faces, in pits located about midpoint between their eyes and nostrils. We assume they detect infrared radiation and by measuring the difference between the heat being sensed on one side of their face and the heat on the other they can precisely locate their prey (or enemy) and direct their strike with astounding accuracy. The strike is swiftly done, almost too fast for the human eye to follow. It has been suggested that other animals, including dogs, also sense infrared radiation. That would seem logical. Some researchers have, they say, located the detectors in the dog's nose.

When snakes equipped with radiation detectors process heat data it is from close up, as far as we know. Homing in on prey by heat is usually confined to an arc within six feet of the snake's head. If the prey animal stumbles away before it dies, the snake follows it using its sense of smell and possibly its Jacobson's organ. If snakes also judge different radiating sources from far away, like the sun, we don't know it yet. It would be useful to them in interpreting the weather because it would give them a chance to locate cover before ambient temperatures rose too high when they were in the open. Snakes are extremely sensitive to heat and can easily be killed by it. However, that is all speculation.

Similarly, we don't know how dogs/wolves use infrared information. Perhaps in winter they can locate small sustaining prey like voles and lemmings even when the little animals are using tunnels under the snow.

Speculation? Yes, but not wildly so. If, in fact, dogs can receive and process information in the infrared part of the spectrum, what about other ranges like ultraviolet? I don't know, of course, but it is a question that has to be asked.

A collie "working" sheep.

We use relatively little of the color spectrum for vision. There is so much more in that continuum that we can detect only with instruments even though part of it, like the infrared part, is giving us skin cancer.

One of the most amazing examples of dog behavior I have ever personally witnessed was exhibited by a random-bred, almost German shepherd bitch named Sheba. I heard about her from the Delta Society, a collection of most wonderful people who match dogs and exceptional people who need a little extra help negotiating their way through our frenetic, demanding world. They told me the astounding story of Sheba and her human charge, Angie. I was so intrigued by what they told me, it was so unbelievable, in fact, that I flew from New York to Washington state and recorded it for network television. It appeared on ABC's "World News Tonight."

Angie is the daughter of a serviceman who was stationed in Germany when Angie was an infant. The little girl came down with a dangerously high fever which began spiking near the lethal range of one hundred and seven day after day. Army doctors tried everything they knew, but they could neither explain the attacks nor halt them. By the time her distraught parents got Angie back to the States, the neurological harm was done. Angie suffers from seizures. Thirteen different kinds were eventually identified. Epilepsy is just one of them.

During some of her attacks Angie stops breathing and her family, mother, father, and two brothers, have had to learn and use CPR. The attacks also mean that Angie can never be left alone. As she was growing up, Angie's parents had to take shifts sitting by her bed all night listening for her breathing. She has as many as a dozen seizures in twenty-four hours, so the vigil is constant around the clock.

When I met Angie she was in her early teens. She is a very pretty girl with a cheery, upbeat personality despite the hell she has lived through. She doesn't know from one moment to the next when she will fall to the floor in uncontrollable spasms, when she will stop breathing and have to rely on other people to keep her alive. She has been near death so many times no one is counting.

There didn't seem to be any relief in sight for Angie or her family. Unfortunately, the constant monitoring of Angie's condition had to extend to the bathroom. If her parents were out, one of her brothers had to be on deck when Angie used the bathroom to bathe or whatever. That has to be hard on a teenage girl.

Switch focus for a minute. The Delta Society has helped establish an aid program in a Washington state penitentiary for women. It is a typical Delta Society program. Women whose lives have been a shambles could learn a skill, have an overwhelming interest and enthusiasm added to their lives, and have the great satisfaction of doing something constructive for other people. They are able to bridge out of themselves and care about something beyond their own instant gratification. That was usually what got them into a mess in the first place. Delta found the experts who would voluntarily go into the prison on a regular basis and train the women to train dogs.

The dogs that come out of the Pullman program are custom-trained for special people. Some pull wheelchairs, some are hearing dogs for the hearing impaired, some answer doors and bring the telephone handset when the phone rings. They do all kinds of things—everything, really, except guiding the visually impaired. There are, of course, excellent programs for those dogs already in place.

Somehow Angie's parents learned of the program and applied for a dog trained to help meet Angie's special needs. The outside experts sat down with the inmate trainers and came to a conclusion that the problems were just too complex. No dog could possibly learn what had to be done. No one knew, really, what they wanted a dog to do. Angie's doctors are barely able to keep up with their part of it. How could a dog be plugged in?

It was decided, however, that Angie would gain emotional benefits from a pet, a simple companion dog. Her social activities are necessarily limited. Angie's mother began taking her to the penitentiary on a regular schedule to participate in the obedience training of Sheba. What everyone felt would be an ideal companion had been located and Sheba was Angie's dog.

The little dog—and Sheba is only about half the size of a German shepherd, about coyote size—took to her training with enthusiasm. Today she is a very well-mannered housedog. But there is something more, much more. It is the closest thing to a miracle I have ever seen. I have heard no explanation for what happened next, none. No one even tries. I would hesitate to put this story in print if my camera crew hadn't recorded the whole thing, everything I am going to describe, and it hadn't appeared on the highest rated network news show in America.

Sheba picked up on Angie's problems. That which the dog could not be trained to do she did herself, perfectly, completely. Sheba is never away from Angie's side. She is always watching Angie and in some way monitoring her health. Whether she does this by smell, sight, sound or very possibly *infrared detection* is impossible to say. Maybe all three of them and maybe some others, too. The infrared, the heat part, is at least likely because a person about to have a seizure has a sudden fever, a quick spike in body temperature. There must also be a change in odor. Somehow, though, that little dog knows before it strikes that Angie is about to be seized. She barks, fusses, grabs Angie's hand in her mouth, and pulls her toward a couch or bed *so Angie doesn't fall on the floor!* Figure out how a dog understands that. Please write me if you do.

One day when we were there, and fortunately we had the camera and lights in place, Angie had a seizure in the living room. I am sorry that Angie had the seizure, but happy that we were in position to record the remarkable behavior of this exceptional dog. Before the onset, Sheba became restive and then started to bark. She grabbed Angie's hand and began backing toward the couch. Very calmly, Angie's mother said, "Go on, Angie, do what Sheba tells you." Within thirty seconds of Angie's lying down and assuming the fetal position the seizure occurred. Her mother put a quilt over her and left the room to check something she had on the stove. She didn't stay to hear if her daughter was still breathing. She didn't have to.

This is perhaps the most astounding part of it. As soon as Angie was curled up on the couch, Sheba jumped up, pushed her way in beside her and cocked her head, keeping her ear next to Angie's nose and mouth. Angie's mother knew that if her daughter's breathing in any way faltered, Sheba would detect it even quicker than she could and give the alarm.

Later that same day, when Angie was in her bedroom, my crew and I were having coffee with her parents at the kitchen table. We heard barking and Sheba came running in, skidded a U-turn, and raced back to the bedroom.

Angie's father said, "I'll go," and followed the dog who was still giving the alarm.

Angie's mother explained, "Angie's breathing is okay, but she may be on the floor. Sheba has a different bark when there are breathing problems. She is much more frantic than that."

We must ask ourselves, does the conventional view of the companion dog provide explanations for Sheba? It is true, the human species throws the occasional genius, the dog species presumably could, too. Even allowing for that, that Sheba is an actual wonder dog, she still has to have the sensory equipment to do the things she does, make the determinations she makes every day.

I watched Angie and Sheba walk down the beach near her home. Sheba was wearing a specially made pack with pockets on the sides carrying the medication Angie must always have on hand. Angie can now take walks, play outside, as long as Sheba is there. I watched them walk away. Our cameraman was off to the side, shuffling along in the dunes, taping them.

"What am I seeing here?" I asked myself. "I have spent my life with dogs and other animals, and I have no explanation for any of this. Nothing I know can account for this."

And, you know I was right. Nothing I have ever heard can explain what happens every day between that lovely little girl, not so little now, and that incredible dog. Anyone who believes that our conventional view of dogs covers this case just hasn't thought much about it.

Where are we now, then? There are the five senses we all have, the extra one dogs have because they have Jacobson's organ, and the probables—magnetic field sensitivity, a means for monitoring barometric pressure, something they appear to use to sense seismic activity before the quake hits, acute awareness of infrared radiation, and whatever Sheba has in combination or well beyond our ken. Readily do I admit that everything on that list after Jacobson's organ, air-tasting, is speculation. I can't quantify anything except my own utter astonishment over things like the team of Angie and Sheba. So we are clearly speculating. The trouble is, Sheba takes us off the end of the chart.

Once, in a discussion on extraterrestrial life, I made the observation that logically the burden of proof lies not with the people who say there is life on other planets, but on those who say there is not. I can say, "There is life in the cosmos," and prove it because I am here to say it and you are here to hear it. Ergo, case proven. Now, if you do not believe that some kind of life exists on many of the billions of other planets, you have to prove the limitation you are imposing. "But it only exists here because _____" Go on, prove it. I'm listening. Life exists in the cosmos, I insist, although I don't know where besides here, or in how many places, perhaps millions of places.

There is no urgency for me to know the answers to those things. All that understanding will come in time. I have two children and four grandchildren. I have installed genes of my own in the future to receive the knowledge. There is never any reason to be frantic about things like this. We are not talking about a vaccine for AIDS.

I believe the same kind of really very simple logic can be used in the discussion of dogs' senses. We know the dog has six senses and I wager that most people who have known dogs will assume there are more. But how many more? Once we open the floodgates and accept that there are more than six, where is the logic of an arbitrary limit? And wouldn't any limit be arbitrary, given the state of our knowledge? If there are seven or eight distinctly different senses, and that seems very likely just with the evidence at hand, what law or reasonable process of thinking says there aren't thirty-seven or thirty-eight—or more or fewer? What would set the limit, based on what we know now? Nothing I know about.

We, our sciences, have actually spent very little money

and time on interpreting animal behavior. We have spent
billions of dollars and millions of man-hours getting someone on the moon. And, indeed, we should have. We have
spent billions of dollars on cancer research, on oil pros-
pecting techniques, on the study of subatomic particles,
and again we should have. One giant particle accelerator
like the four-mile tunnel in Batavia, Illinois, at the Fermi
Laboratory, used to study antimatter and things like that,
or one giant reflecting telescope used to probe outer space
costs more in dollars and man-hours than has been spent
in all time on the study of dog behavior. That is as it should
be.

I don't think that our priorities are misplaced at all in
this regard. But we have to stop thinking as if the state of
science in astronautics, medicine, desalinization, genetic
engineering, or in any other discipline suggests a level
where our knowledge of animals is today. Science does
not move forward in a solid rank, with a nice clean leading
edge. Science looks like the edge of a ragged saw magnified
a thousand times. There are peaks and very deep valleys.
Whatever kind of whiz kids we may be in some sciences,
when it comes to understanding animal behavior we are
deep, deep down in a valley. We are way behind many
other sciences. Again, that's okay. Someday we will catch
up. All we are doing here is speculating on what we are
going to find as we do.

Desmond Morris suggests a simple explanation for yet
another canine phenomenon. He speaks of someone who
says his or her dog "has seen a ghost." He says that is due
in all probability to a strong scent deposit or something
coming to the animal's nose on the wind. He suggests that
what Oomiac did that night long ago out near the tip of
New York's Long Island was just that, not "seeing a ghost"
but smelling something that intrigued or upset her. Well,
it wasn't a scent *deposit* because she did not try to locate
it. She didn't drop her head and sniff the ground and she
didn't appear to be at all anxious to go forward or to either

side to find one. If it was scent, it was almost certainly windborne.

As for the ghost part of it; no sir, no ma'am, no way. I wouldn't touch that one for any price. I don't know what a ghost is or is supposed to be, not really, and I try to avoid discussing things in public that rightly or wrongly carry the label of "nut." Do I privately believe in ghosts? Certainly not. Do I disbelieve in ghosts? Certainly not. I am fortunate. I don't have to take a stand. And I am far too ignorant in this regard to even think of one.

Again, there is nothing wrong with transient ignorance unless you are trying to cure or avoid something bad. People should be comfortable with ignorance in some categories where an emergency is not demonstrable. We should work on overcoming it, to be sure. When we suffer from it we can reasonably expect our children, or theirs, or theirs, etc., will not be.

I don't know what happened to Oomiac that night and by extension to me. I do know that it was not an academic exercise. It was real, it was more than just a little chilling, and it was confounding. I don't think it was smell. Anything that could have crossed our paths had done so before, many times. This wasn't an African or Asian wilderness, it was an American seaside countryside fast becoming far too suburban for my tastes. Oomiac had already lived there for years. There were no great electrifying surprises to experience that I can imagine. Yet something, somehow, through some avenue, possibly one we don't yet know about, absolutely riveted that dog. I have watched dogs interact, and react with and to, the world around us all of my life, as child and adult. There are two dogs within two feet of me as I make these observations. As an experienced observer, if not an expert one, something really got to that Siberian husky that night. It was something that was, at least in her mind, big doings. It was, in the current vernacular, pretty heavy out there that night. I will leave it at that.

• •

There is one other aspect to all of this that we should consider. In prescribing medication your doctor and your pharmacist have to take into account the matter of synergisms. Some drugs react with each other to enhance the effect one or the other has on a human being. A normal dose of barbiturates can be lethal when the drug alcohol is added in a person's system. When drugs act to negate each other's effects it is called antagonism.

Synergisms are very complex in any form. We should ponder that. What if a number of senses acting together have what we could refer to as a synergistic effect on each other? That could account for a condition requiring a new definition, or provide a sensory mode almost worthy of being called a new sense. An example: a dog approaches the carcass of a deer left by a hunter in the woods. (It happens in our woods with our dogs all the time, in season and out.) Consider this situation.

The dog approaching the carcass is directed by his nose. How much of a role Jacobson's organ has in all of this is not fully understood. Characteristically, the dog will be cautious. He will look around and listen to determine if there is going to be a challenge from another animal. That is genetically programmed. Where there is food there very well may be a fight. If the coast is clear the dog will smell the carcass and perhaps push it with his nose to get more scent particles swirling around to take in and analyze. He may paw it. Again, we assume the Jacobson's organ is working in concert. If the dog's brain says he should taste the carcass, he will take a first, tentative bite. His tongue will determine texture by the sense of touch and the animal's saliva will carry chemical information to taste buds toward the rear of the tongue for analysis and the relay of data to the brain. Unless the dog is ravenously hungry, that is about how it will go. There is a lot of interplay even in that simple scenario. If there are other senses at work, we cannot yet define them.

What kind of a synergistic role may these simultaneous sensing patterns have on each other? What one sense, if it were lost, would cause the animal to turn away? Perhaps any one of them except sight and hearing. Blind and deaf dogs eat just as enthusiastically as sighted and hearing dogs. We have had both.

In summary, we don't know how many senses a dog has. That means we don't really know how he relates to his surroundings. We don't know except in the most rudimentary way how a dog's senses, those we can identify and those we cannot, overlay and interact with each other. As for the dog on the deer carcass, if you are a witness, and the dog is feeding, could he only learn of your presence by seeing you or hearing you or interpreting any odor you were able to originate that was strong enough to intrude on the smell of the carcass? I don't know, but I suspect there are other ways for the animal to monitor what was going on around him. It may be some time before we really understand all of that, before we really understand our canine friends.

8

WITHOUT ANY apologies, I love our dogs. I really do, after the fashion of my own species. And they love me, I am sure, in the way dogs do that kind of thing. I don't suggest that we love each other in the same way, not at all. I tend to think that if dogs possessed nothing more than a duplicate of our emotional and intellectual packages we would have tired of them as companions long ago. They wouldn't have come all this distance with us. We would not have cherished their companionship enough to feed them, to care for them.

In an economic sense, not an emotional one certainly, fewer dogs have earned their keep than have not. They are not four-legged, relatively slow people. They are wolf/dogs, members of a very different line of ascent on the mammalian evolutionary tree. It is miraculous that our two lines have blended so well and that we jointly can form such a rewarding community.

We are party to a most interesting combination. It is satisfying, I believe, at least in part because dogs are children that are never quite able to grow up no matter how smart they are. And so they always make us feel important and needed. We are. We always have our place with them. And we know what that place is, in contrast to our relationship with many of the members of our own species that we encounter in life. That is one reason the report of a dog bite is so unpleasant, so troublesome to the people close to the situation. It is a betrayal of a basic understanding dogs and man have been living by since very ancient times, perhaps for two hundred centuries. It is a breach of contract. What is it, then, I wonder, when we abuse or neglect them?

Any discussion of how and what dogs may feel as emotions has to be almost entirely anecdotal. The same holds true for their intellect, which we'll discuss later. I will admit that anecdotes do not a science make. But anecdotes are often what sets a science on its path of discovery. A volcanic event is an anecdote, so is an earthquake, an attack of appendicitis, a tornado, a birth, a mating, a change of seasons, a predator stalk and kill; all are anecdotes, but all have appropriate sciences that can readily place them in a meaningful context for study and understanding. We could be secure in discussing any of them, but that is not our mission. We are trying to squish ourselves inside a dog's skull.

If a scientific context for explanation has not been established, however, it does not mean that the anecdotes didn't occur. We really don't have the luxury of shelving something just because we haven't established a niche for it. If people were not already in the business of studying volcanoes with computers and seismic sounds, etc., could we have said to Mount St. Helens after her recent escapades:

"Sorry, we aren't set up for your carryings-on. Just go away and pretend you never happened. Cool those rumbles in your tummy until we invent a science sometime in the next century to deal with them."

It would be a grand intellectual luxury if we could take things as we wanted to rather than as they came along. We do not have that luxury, however, and should never have pretended that we did. There is an urgency to our learning about animal effect and cognition and that will

become evident as we move along in this chapter.

An anecdote: Zack is a fine specimen of a yellow Labrador retriever. He is thumping, solid dog whose endlessly wagging tail can sweep a coffee table clean or give you an attention-getting whack on the shins. Annie is a Jack Russell terrier who is as large of heart as she is small in size. They are two of the four dogs that now live with my daughter Pamela and her husband, Joe. The other two dogs are Luke, the golden greyhound with the eyes of a doe, and dear little Chloe Sweetpea, the three-legged dog we discussed earlier. It is a harmonious community—two adults, two little girls, Sarah and Hannah, the four dogs and a half-a-dozen cats, a pony, and a burro. An odd gerbil or hamster brought on board the ark isn't really part of the community. That category of beast must be securely contained and isolated because of the other animals. Rodents are not so much neighbors as they are sporting challenges for cats, of course, but no less so for terriers and sight hounds.

Pamela is an executive and simply has to travel. Joe is in the Maryland National Guard and was called up when Iraq went from irksome to intolerable. Suddenly the world changed in the Rupert household. The girls have their nanny and they also spend a great deal of time here at Thistle Hill Farm with us. And because they are the oldest two Rupert dogs and seem to suffer more, Annie and Zack often come here, too. On a farm where there are already ten dogs, two more hardly matter.

We have a community of animals here and any real fighting has to be out of the question. Everybody seems to understand that imperative; the cats seldom get chased and then only in fun. They seem to enjoy the romp as much as the dogs do when it does happen, when spirits are higher than usual. How do we know that? Because whenever they feel like knocking it off the targeted cats sit down and whack any dog that comes near them. The dogs then go off and invent another, safer game. The cats didn't have to tolerate it at all if they hadn't wanted to. And at night the dogs and cats frequently curl up together, which doesn't indicate terror on either's part. Dogs can be pains, ask any cat, but they also make pretty good hot water bottles.

Rarely is there a squabble among the dogs themselves. There has been, of course, but the event brought such thundering disapproval at the time it happened that it has not often been repeated. Greyhounds just don't fight and the others know perfectly well how to make their annoyance known to each other far short of actually throwing tantrums.

Zack's universe centers squarely on Joe. He is a fine dog with Pamela and the girls, wonderful with anyone or anything that comes through the door. But Joe is something else again. Annie the Jack Russell is the same way about Pamela. Pamela is the focal point of the cosmos. Zack is never willingly out of sight of Joe, and Annie is a limpet attached to Pamela. Anyone who has lived with dogs has seen this kind of thing. As gregarious and as sociable as a dog may be, there is very often one person who is *IT*. I believe that that in itself, the undeniable expression of preference, indicates choice, and therefore thought, and therefore intelligence, all the way unto cognition.

When Joe went on active duty with the Guard, Zack obviously couldn't understand. He stood by the door, he waited or he paced, and stopped frequently and appeared to be listening. We do not know, of course, what else he was doing. To say that Zack wasn't feeling some kind of emotional trauma is absurd. He suffered. When Joe got his first weekend off and came home Zack sat next to his chair, rested his chin on Joe's knee, and closed his eyes. He didn't move and I am sure he didn't want Joe to, either. He wasn't asking to be petted, he wasn't asking for food. He had missed Joe terribly and when he got him back he just wanted to soak up the pleasure of the moment. All of his actions seemed to indicate that he had been thinking about Joe and, who knows, perhaps worrying in some way.

While Joe was away Pamela had a business conference she simply had to attend. It had been scheduled a year in advance and there was no way out of it. The girls came here with Annie and Zack and it is hard to tell which of the dogs was in a worse funk. Annie sulked and Zack moped. The girls played and were as happy as clams. The dogs were not as adjustable. Annie lay on a chaise lounge and stared straight ahead. Someone or something had poked a hole in her universe and she was trying to sort it all out. Zack just looked glum. He went to the door every few minutes and, again, apparently listened. At night we had to keep our bedroom door open so we could hear the kids in the nursery. We could hear poor old Zack pacing. He just couldn't settle down. His world was in disarray and, to project a bit, it seemed as if his heart would break.

What was the emotion or, perhaps plural, what were the emotions involved? The dogs were *sad,* they *missed* their master and mistress, they were *confused* because their neat, dependable world had inexplicably become messy and undependable? Could the dogs have felt *rejected, unwanted, cast off, set aside, abandoned*? Could they have felt *guilt* the way children often do in divorce cases or parental deaths? Could there have been some shadowy feeling of *fault*? Dogs certainly look guilty when they are caught with their manners down. Perhaps none of those words really work. I suspect that when we do begin sorting out the mysteries of animal emotions we may find that an entirely new vocabulary will be needed. I note with interest that when Dr. Jane Goodall writes so enchantingly and revealingly of her thirty years of field work with chimpanzees at Gombe in Tanzania, she does not appear to hesitate to use the same words to describe the moods of the chimpanzees' inner world we would use to describe our own. We may not have the appropriate words, but that does not mean that the wild chimpanzees of Gombe or our domestic dogs do not have genuine emotional feelings. The failure, if such there is in this matter, is ours not theirs.

When we entered the nuclear age and later the space age vast new vocabularies were needed. And now it is happening again with genetics and genetic engineering, not to mention computers. Today, barely moments after these new ages were born, we have enough new words for each of them to fill a dictionary and that is literally true. The dictionaries, in fact, have already been published. I think we may have to see that happen again when deep probes are made not into space and not into the heart of the atom or DNA, but into the heart of the dog. I don't have a new word for Zack's condition, so for the moment I guess we just have to say that he was sad. Therein lies a paradox. When we speak of nuclear forces, of DNA, of this computer's innards, of space exploration, we wouldn't dream of using old language from other intellectual watersheds. When we try to understand a dog's mind, we do.

Apparently dogs suffer from depression and perhaps it can get so bad that it would be clinical in a human being. We speak of dogs being hyperkinetic. Dogs suffering from that condition are extremely difficult to live with. Heaven help them, and us, since they have a lifelong paradoxical reaction to medication like phenobarbital, just as kids do up until puberty. It can be very wearing and some dogs that suffer from hyperkinesis become biters. Their reactions are disastrously inappropriate, in some cases, to just about everything that happens around them. Offering them a biscuit with your fingers is downright hazardous. They are murder with other animals. That comes close to describing the manic phase of manic/depression in people. It is seen in a great deal of criminal behavior, as well. It is almost a hallmark in many forms of social pathology.

Is there an analog here? Can dogs, too, be manic depressives? They can act as if they are. Very often they are put to sleep when they become too much of a trial in the home. It seems a shame, but no one seems to have the answer. Off the wall is off the wall in man or dog and the symptoms are not always that different.

There really isn't much in the way of psychiatric help available for dogs, except in a few isolated places and then only of sorts. Unfortunately, when it is offered as a science it is often, but perhaps not always, a rip-off. Most dogs that have problems just have to suffer through them as well as they can. It helps to have tolerant, gentle and understanding human members of the pack. Perhaps, since their minds are almost certainly less complex than our own, dogs suffer from fewer complaints than we do and perhaps their illnesses are not as complicated as ours, or maybe their awareness of them is mercifully shallow. We don't have any real answers yet, but I do know that dogs can be hyper, slothlike, sad, far too aggressive, very submissive, timid to the point of fear, biting, silly, inflexible, unable to adapt, stubborn, uncooperative, asocial, inappropriate, embarrassed and embarrassing, out-of-line in many ways including being destructive and even seriously dangerous. Dogs can also be solid friends, reliable, joyfully gregarious, secure, warm and understanding (or so it seems), supportive (that may be us reacting to them, not really them at all), and seemingly wise. All of those descriptive words, both the positive ones and the negative, were developed for human conditions and as we said there are no really satisfactory linguistic analogs for animal moods and behavior, yet. In time, I am confident, there will be. In the meantime, suffice it to say that sadness has to have roots in awareness unless it is truly pathological.

A couple of the old bromides I have heard repeated since I was a boy are that animals don't have a sense of self and

Male and female Greek greyhounds, second century A.D.

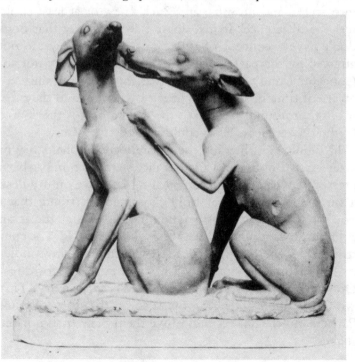

they don't have a sense of time. Now how do you suppose
we could possibly know that? In fact, we don't know that
at all. They are part and parcel of that old offhand descrip-
tion we once seemed compelled to use to make ourselves
comfortably aloof. And why, do you suppose, we would
want to feel aloof? From each other, okay, but from our
dogs! That is the most self-defeating kind of relationship
imaginable. We have nonjudgmental all-trusting pets so
we can relate to them without stress. Why would we then
want to remain aloof from them? Aloofness is the antithesis
of easy, reassuring companionship.

Zack was used to seeing both Pamela and Joe go off to
work five days a week. Once a month Joe would be away
with the National Guard for a weekend. Zack was always
delighted to get Joe back, but it was not much more of a
show than that. There was no real *sturm und drang*. This
time, however, the days stretched out one after the other
into weeks and months, and Zack knew or at least could
feel the difference. It just doesn't work to say that dogs
don't have a concept of time. That implies they are not
affected by the passage of time and that is simply not so.
Concept? I don't know about that, but they certainly are
aware of time in some way, their own way, and they feel
it often profoundly. Perhaps the feeling of it is the source
of their awareness. That could also be true of us.

In Edinburgh they tell the possibly apocryphal story of
Greyfriar's Bobby, and a rather nice statue to him has been
erected as well. As I sit here writing I can see on my desk
a small reproduction of Bobby's memorial tribute that I
bought when I was last in Edinburgh. The statue is an
Edinburgh landmark. Everybody knows it. It was contributed by the Baroness Burdett-Coutts. It is on Candle-
maker's Row and sits atop a fountain put there for dogs.
Don't ask anyone in Edinburgh if this is a true story. That
would be like challenging the Irish on the story of Saint
Patrick and the snakes, God love them. The Irish not the
snakes.

Very briefly, Bobby was a faithful pet who lost his master when he was still a relatively young dog. That would have been about 1858. Heartbroken, as the story goes, Bobby followed the funeral procession to the church and when the services were over and everybody had gone about their own affairs the sad little dog lay down on his master's grave. There he stayed until his own death fourteen years later, in 1872. Friends whose names are recorded and who were obviously real people, not fictional ones, brought him food and water, but winter and summer Bobby stayed there, perhaps waiting, perhaps guarding his master's grave. Tourists came to visit him from as far away as the United States. He was very famous by the time he died and he was, according to the story, given special dispensation and buried next to his master. The Scots do love their dogs and Bobby was a dog the Scots still love most especially to this day.

The wonderful story of the faithful Bobby may be true in part and it could be at least partly exaggerated. I suppose it could be all true, or it may be cut from whole cloth and be just another lovely fictional story of what goes on between us and our dogs. There are many such tales that have come down to us all over the world, often in the most unexpected places. I don't think it matters all that much if the story of Greyfriar's Bobby is a true account of actual historical events. There is the statue and a lot of people have believed it and it sells a lot of postcards and miniature statues like the one I bought. Personally, I like such stories because they cast the dog in a positive light. All of the animals on earth, wild and domestic, have such a tough road with us in charge that anything that can give them good press is all to their good and we should be supportive of that goal.

The point about Greyfriar's Bobby—Greyfriar's is the name of the graveyard—is that true or false or a little bit of both, it reflects facts that people have been observing about their own dogs for a long time. Their faithfulness and their apparent emotional attachment to us have been reality for millions and millions of people for a good many thousands of years. They are, as the current expression goes, givens. Bobby has been a kind of last word in faithfulness even if his story is symbolic more than actually true as told. Again, though, we really do not know.

It is possible to find these same themes running through the world's symbology, tradition, and literature like a *leit motif.* If we approach these fables and legends as an anthropologist might we can discern a foundation for our considerations here.

Point 1: Men and women have had real life experiences with domestic dogs descended from wolves for millennia.

Point 2: Men and women have kept alive in their storytelling the ideas that dogs are intelligent, keen, alert, ever true. They are pictured as noble companions.

Point 3: Cultural anthropologists tell us we must never ignore fables, legends and tales because they contain an enormous amount of information about what a culture has experienced as it evolved. Cultures, like people, are the sum total of where they have been and what they have been through, and that includes a very diagnostic constituent called lore. Lore may often be imaginative, but it is not accidental, nor is it ignorable.

Only a very shallow-minded person, perhaps an arrogant fool, in fact, would dare cast aside all traditional knowledge as useless nonsense. Tradition, oral and written, are windows into the historical soul of a people. They are fountains of knowledge and we should drink of them and thereby grow if not wise then at least better informed and perhaps, insofar as it suits us, a wee bit humble. There is an awful lot about dogs and their cognitive abilities, if not powers, in the world's traditional knowledge. It didn't come to be there by chance, nor did one person invent it. It is well founded in peoples' experiences.

The timeless quality of a dog's faithfulness and patience was reported as far back as the eighth century B.C. when

A third century A.D. Roman sarcophagus, with greyhound.

Homer wrote of the faithful hound Argos in the *Odyssey*.
Argos waited for twenty years for Odysseus to return from
the Trojan War. When Odysseus returned, in mufti to
avoid men plotting to kill him so they could have a go at
his wife, Argos looked at him and wagged his tail. The
disguised man could not possibly acknowledge the dog
without giving himself away, although the dog had been
waiting for two decades for that moment of recognition.
Homer reports that Odysseus wept and at that moment
Argos, a neglected and partially crippled old hound, low-
ered his head onto the dung heap where he had been lying
and died.

   I don't believe we can really think of stories like this

from that long ago as anything but legend, but the fact that Homer recorded it at all is interesting. There had to have been a tradition even then about dogs and their sticking power. The fact that Homer has Odysseus the warrior weeping speaks of the bond between animal and man that was already familiar enough for it to have meaning for Homer's original readers. It is one of those elements in a story that has to have had an *underlayment* of understanding and acceptance for it to have been the least bit credible.

If Homer or any other writer had another kind of animal, say a rooster, rat or cobra, wait faithfully for twenty years and then recognize its master, the audience for the tale would be confused. There would be no frame of reference to make the reader comfortable. But nearly three thousand years ago Homer was able to include the story of a faithful dog in his classic epic and get knowing nods of approval and understanding from his readers. He still does. It is comfortably familiar for us, too. Before there is a tale or tradition in a culture there must be in fact some kind of accepted truth, something that is very real and culturally tangible. The kind of faith and nobleness that Homer reported appears again and again in the world's literature and has obviously been a concept with a basis in truth that all kinds of people have been able to relate to.

In 1826, in his novel *Woodstock,* Sir Walter Scott—again in Scotland, you will note—told the story of Bevis, a huge and faithful mastiff. As a young dog, Bevis had saved his master's life and then lived on to comfort him in his old age. There is a warm and touching bond between the old dog and the old man. The only surprising part is that mastiffs have a very short life, rarely as much as ten years. That is true of all of the giant breeds. One wonders if the word *mastiff* was being used in some general way and was not specific to the breed we know by that name today. There is a lot of that in any history, the changing meanings and values of words.

In a story written much more recently, in 1945, a splen-

did showdog, an Irish setter named Big Red, saves sev-
enteen-year-old Danny Pickett from a rogue bear, sustaining such serious injuries in the encounter that they put
an end to his show career. That was in the novel *Big Red*
by Jim Kjelgaard. Again, audiences could relate to the story
because of what they already knew of dogs and not just
incidentally because Irish setters were so popular at the
time.

Ludwig Bemelmans has Bosy, a Bouvier des Flandres,
climbing a ladder to save a doll and then, on a second
ascent, carrying a terrified cat from a burning building in
The World of Ludwig Bemelmans (1955). Rudyard Kipling
has the dog Boots mourn for a canine friend in *Thy Servant
a Dog* (1930). Tradition, not literature, has Keeper, Emily
Bronte's dog, attending her funeral, sitting in the family
pew, and then stationing himself outside her bedroom door
and whining for weeks. All of these stories, fact or fiction,
and all that we experience ourselves as fact, reinforce each
other and our faith in something very old and very real

to us. It is also, we must admit, something very precious.

In Muslim lore (and this is a really surprising place to find such a story, as we will see) Kitmit stays awake for three hundred and nine years to keep watch outside a cave where God was in hiding to avoid persecution. The surprising part arises from the fact that Muslims have a strong traditional hatred for most dogs. The saluki they love, but they really have a terrible prejudice against just about all other breeds. Yet even in the complicated world of Islam there is a faithful dog, although three hundred and nine years does stretch even my willingness to believe in anything good about dogs.

Back to some current anecdotes regarding our dogs' feelings. *Feeling* can mean a number of things, everything from intuition or a hunch—based perhaps on sensory systems as yet unidentified—to pleasure and pain and all that they imply as reactions to stimuli. That stimuli can be another creature of our own or another species, so that is where our emotions get semantically parked.

Does your dog have a sense of humor? Some of mine have it while others, perfectly nice dogs, mind you, are or were without one. Duncan doesn't appear to have one. He is always serious because as a herding dog he believes very strongly that his responsibilities should occupy all of his waking hours. He is a watchdog, he herds the cats and the other dogs, he worries about the horses, he worries about us. If he didn't have other outlets I swear he would herd the toilet and bathtub. He is a very nice dog, a splendid companion on a walk in the meadow or the woods, very obedient, but there is no humor about him at all unless you are amused by how serious he is. His one big game is soccer. He has a large boomer ball about a foot in diameter. He chases it for hours on end, propelling it up and down hills with his nose, barking furiously at it all the while. He does that to have something to herd, of course. He has invented his own flock of sheep. Unfortunately, it has to be confiscated during the summer. One pass with that heavy ball pursued by Duncan can wipe out hours of work in a flower bed or vegetable garden. Before we decided that border-collie soccer was an off-season game you could tell when Duncan was making a pass through the vegetable garden by the tomatoes becoming airborne in a straight line right through the middle of all that loving work and attention.

Duncan is as dour as any other Scot. In fact, his mother was a Scot who was purchased in the Highlands by Clint Rowe and brought back to Hollywood for an arrangement with Mike. But then there was Brigitte Petite Noir—my beloved Biddie.

Brigitte was a black toy poodle and was the third jewel in the crown, one of my three favorite dogs of all time. Now, there was a sense of humor! She was vain and she knew it and she laughed at herself. She could play the game with perfect abandon. She was with it, no other way can it be put, she realized full well how silly a place the world is and, well, she was with it. It was fine with her because she got everything she wanted out of life.

Once about every six weeks a very pleasant wisp of a young man, native of a soft and gentle place where the

offal of the world smells like potpourri, I am sure, would manifest himself at our door and carry the unresisting Biddie away to his van, clutching her to his breast and cooing. Later that same day she would reappear, bathed, coiffed and all-over smartened. I never was able to deter the beautician from the fingernail polish and ribbon bit. No matter how intense my prohibitions, Brigitte would reappear as if both she and her beauty consultant had popped out from under a toadstool, she wearing a ribbon in her topknot that had been carefully color-coordinated with the fingernail polish chosen for that day and evident on all of her nails. I can't imagine what Biddie and the fair young man talked about while all of this was being done, but Biddie adored him and never minded going off in the van that led to her glory.

The important point is that Biddie thought it was uproariously funny. No matter which way you turned that evening, Biddie was posing, doing model turns, receiving the admiration of all. She jumped up on chairs when she heard anyone coming and stood there waiting to be examined and praised. When the adoration seemed to be flagging, she held out a paw and showed you her nails. She knew that was always good for a rise. She loved it, the little hussy—her behavior on the evening she came from the beauty parlor was markedly different from any other evening. She wallowed in praise and admiration and she damn well knew how silly it was. She was simply playing the game with the rest of us. Very often she was sent off to the parlor of her improvement when there was going to be a party or gathering of some sort that evening. With a house full of people available for her ego gratification the posturing became so intense she would sometimes have to be banished to a bedroom.

Biddie and I had a trick, a kind of parlor game. I would hypnotize her. It was like the old comic shtick where the comedian flops his head to the side as if falling instantly asleep. Biddie would sit on my lap with her little fore-

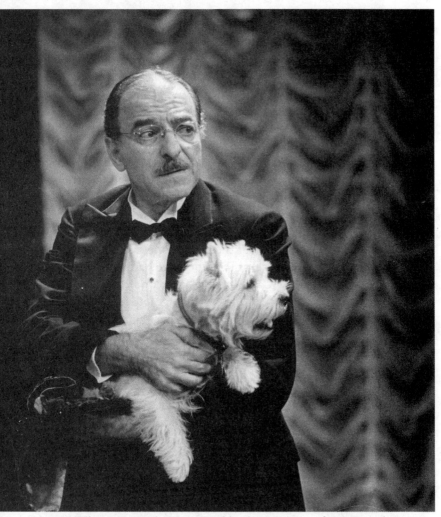

Actor Willie Brown (the West Highland terrier) is a favorite at the Long Wharf Theater in New Haven, Connecticut. He appears in Dinner at Eight *with Clement Fowler.*

paws on my chest and I would start the routine:

"*Brigitte Petite Noir,*" I would intone, "*look into my eyes. You are getting sleepy. You are falling asleep, your eyes are getting heavy. Now sleep until I awaken you.*"

At that point Biddie would flop her head against my

chest with her eyes closed. It really was very funny and as I look back I never felt silly doing it. It wasn't silly, really, it was a little bit of vaudeville in the parlor. It never failed to get approval from the crowd, whether they had seen it done before or not. As a matter of fact, scores of times the performances were done on request or command. I always feel good when I am interacting with a dog so I liked it, and Biddie simply adored it because she got attention. If the conversation went on too long without in some way involving her Biddie would jump up into my lap and assume the position. If I ignored her she did her part of the act without me. She would do it again and again until she got the focus of the room where she felt it should be. Again, there were times when she had to be banished.

Anyone who saw that little poodle and didn't think she had a sense of humor didn't have one themselves. It existed in her every posture, her every move, very nearly.

A humorous sidebar; during Biddie's time with us there was another dog on deck, six or seven times her size at least, named Nel Gwynn. She was a rescue case I had found nearly dead from starvation on a New York City street, apparently German shepherd, airedale, plus whatever else the gods had chosen for this unique mix, in a word, random-bred. She was a wonderful dog all the days of her life and very protective of our then small kids.

At that time Jill's grandmother lived with us and at ninety she could be a bit forgetful and often very stubborn. One day when Jill and I were going out we told her that he of the ribbon and fingernail polish would be coming by for Brigitte and to just let him take her. But when the man appeared at the door, poor Mrs. Langdon became very confused. She absolutely insisted that we had left strict instructions that rangy old Nel was to go and not Brigitte. Bewildered but unable to sway the old lady, and apparently afraid to tackle her physically, he went off with the very confused Nel while Brigitte, I am sure, stamped her paw in rage. That evening we had a sulking and disgruntled toy poodle and a very inappropriately adorned random-bred pooch who looked absolutely absurd with fingernail polish. She had no topknot, so there was no ribbon. Thank heavens for small favors.

What glands made Brigitte the adorable little clown she was almost to the day of her death yet made Duncan, although affectionate with me, so very serious about honor, service, and duty? Breeding, of course; they were bred for different characteristics. Yet I am sure there have been herding dogs with humor and poodles without the great gift. The first dog Jill and I got, just a year after we were married, was a miniature poodle named—heaven help us—Tutu. He was a rotten puppy who grew up to be a rotten dog. He had no sense of humor and a foul disposition. We finally gave him away after trying every trick there was to salvage him. He bit Jill, he bit me, still we hated to admit defeat and give up on him. Then two-year-old Pamela ran her toy plastic vacuum cleaner over him, all eighteen ounces of it, and he seriously attacked her. One trip for stitches was Tutu's full allowance. He went to a farm in Connecticut where there were no children. I never asked what happened to him after that because if the truth be known I really didn't care. I doubt that the monster made out there either.

Duncan, who would never bite but who won't smile either; Brigitte, who wouldn't have bitten anyone for any reason and who laughed at the world all the time; Tutu, the wretch, who never laughed and bit like a demon—why were they so different? Personality, individuality.

In fact, dogs are individuals and genetics can't account for all of the differences. To the argument that social conditioning could explain what is not explained by genetics I would suggest that an animal has to be intelligent enough to respond to the conditions it encounters if it is to be molded by them. Dogs have different levels of intelligence as members of different breeds (that would be genetics) and as products of different environments (which would

not be). They also differ in intelligence and personality for exactly the same reason you and I do, and everyone we know does. Some have it and some do not.

For more on the subject of feelings and emotion (are they really the same? I tend to think not), I have, you guessed it, a bit of observed behavior, i.e., another anecdote:

When Chloe Sweetpea, the three-legged puppy, joined my daughter's (and her husband's) household she was very quickly adopted by Luke, the golden greyhound. Within hours she was his. Although he is a male, he has been endlessly broody with his charge, and she often sleeps between his front legs with her chin on his neck where she is probably able to hear the blood in his carotid artery. The rhythm there would be about the same as the one she heard or at least felt in her mother's uterus. Probably felt since a puppy's ears really aren't functional until at least seven to ten days after birth. It can be as long as two weeks. When she isn't sleeping on Luke she is cuddled up near him. They are never far apart. Not for long, at least.

During their playtime together Luke and Chloe Sweetpea tussle constantly. She chews on him and he chews on her, but there is never a mark on either. The funniest sight is when Luke feels like doing laps. He opens up and whips around an acre or two as if possessed. He is a golden blur. The other dogs, Zack the Labrador, et al., have long since learned that it is sheer folly to try to keep up. Mostly they lie down with their back to him, pretending it isn't happening, but not Chloe Sweetpea. On three legs she runs along behind, certain I am sure that she will eventually catch up. Of course, she does, often, every time Luke passes her. Sometimes he stops, panting, and looks back at her. If she has paddled off and is out of sight he immediately comes back to find her. He worries about her, I think. He certainly behaves as though he does.

The anecdote: Missy, my granddaughter's pony, has a new companion, Pedro the burro. Pedro was a feral animal from out West and was captured and sold at auction. He eventually ended up as a pet and was passed around as those poor beasts so often are, but he has now really settled down very well for an animal that was born and lived several years in the wild. He is still highly suspicious of dogs, though, which is a healthy trait for any wild animal. He reflexively kicks any dog that gets near him, no matter what their size or attitude may be. Again, that is native wisdom for a hoofed animal not thoroughly familiar with each individual dog it encounters. Kick first and ask questions later seems to be Pedro's motto in his dealings with anything of the canine kind.

The other day Chloe Sweetpea wandered into the paddock and decided to find out what a donkey smells like up close. Pedro nailed her, knocked her off all three of her legs. As puppies are wont to do, she began screaming and scrambled under the fence, still yowling her misery and surprise in a terrified, shrill voice. Pamela witnessed the sequence and is our reporter. Luke took off like a bullet, running toward his beloved puppy friend. Pamela swears that in the last few feet Luke went down and slid in like a base-stealing ball player. He literally scooped Chloe up in his front legs and pulled her to his chest. He sniffed her all over, licked her, and she played it for all it was worth, whimpering softly until she finally put her chin down on one of Luke's paws and looked around, raising first one eyebrow and then the other. Finally, she took a nap. Pedro brayed.

To deny there is a bond between that altered adult male and that funny little female puppy is silly. Plainly there is. Is it glandular? Did altering Luke after he was rescued from the track—or, more accurately, after his career on the track was over—did that give him new imperatives and make him out-and-out as broody as a bitch? I doubt it. I think Luke loves Chloe Sweetpea and she loves him. Since I can't define love in my own species (I do believe it is more than a glandular disturbance and an opportunity to file joint income tax returns) I won't try to define love among our dogs. But as sure as I am that I love my wife of thirty-seven years, and that she is more than just conditioned to me, so I believe those two dogs at my daughter's place love each other, too. An anecdote, yes, but not all that difficult to place in a context with many, many parallels.

We have come from a time when virtually all of the

world's scientists thought of animals as complex but unthinking robots, devices, variously warm and cold things.
Everybody acknowledged that each one, every individual
and every species, is miraculous to behold but that none
of them either thought thoughts, whatever *they* are, or felt
feelings, again an ill-defined word. Ill-defined? I wonder
if it has been defined at all. What we really are wondering
about is where we are going from here. What will we
someday discover, what will we know about animal emotions and animal cognition? That, of course, is where the
head-scratching comes in. We don't know, not a real clue
do we have, but we do here acknowledge and record the
movement away from that old time of animal robots. Distinctly, we are in the process of leaving all of that behind.

All kinds of things have held us back. Orthodoxy has
made scientists afraid of limbs that had to be gone out
upon, religion has been so strict in its absolute insistence
that animals do not have souls (define your own, please)
that the idea that animals could think and feel (while not
the same thing at all) still has been potentially heretical and
dangerous to our self-mandated superiority. Remember,
the Good Book gives us dominion. Then there are the
activities of man that have made it just about essential that
animals not think and feel. That is perhaps where we have
been hung up the most.

Consider this brief Dickensian story of a dog. There is
an important lesson here that could explain a lot about us
and our fast-fading idea that animals are emotionless,
thoughtless however pleasant robots.

I have mentioned Sirius, the last of the three racing greyhound rescue cases to join our canine pack here at Thistle
Hill Farm. It is of his recent history that I speak.

When the rescue committee made their regular stop at
a track in New Hampshire they were a little low in spirits.
They had only three openings. They already had more
dogs than potential homes. It is a reality of the animal
rescue field that every container can hold just so much and

then you simply have to stop pouring. That is the hardest part of it all, playing God. It is a terrible thing for anyone to have to do. Power sounds like fun until you have it and it involves life and death for creatures you care about. Then it becomes a terrible thing.

The dogs that were presented to the rescue committee as scheduled to die that day were all worthies, all very nice animals, but the rescuers already had more worthies on hand than they knew what to do with. They agonized and decided that by stretching every resource they had in every imaginable direction they could take an absolute maximum of three dogs, although no one was sure how they would manage to do even that. The problem was there were twenty-five lovely dogs all less than four years old, a good many under three. Almost by closing their eyes and pointing, the rescuers indicated three and left the other twenty-two dogs to die later that afternoon.

Sirius was not among the chosen not because he wasn't a potentially wonderful pet but for the reasons already cited—there just wasn't room. Now, Sirius has a strange habit (yes, he is still alive). He rolls his lips back and shows his teeth in a big wide smile. He does it to greet you, he does it when he is about to get a cookie, he does it when you ask him to, he does it when I sing, beautifully, of course, *"There are smiles that make you happy . . ."*

It is one of the ways that Sirius interacts with people. He simply smiles. It is easy enough to understand. A very similar facial expression in wolves is part of the submission ritual. It is in part how a wolf below the Alpha position acknowledges a socially superior animal. Sirius has the same characteristic, but it is just slightly out of sync. It came down to him with his wolf genes, but without the instruction booklet.

One of the rescue committee members got home to find a message on her telephone answering machine asking her to call the veterinarian to whom the twenty-two ill-starred dogs from the track had been taken to be put to sleep.

A greyhound of 1820.

(Isn't it strange how we say euthanized, PTS, put to sleep, put down, all of these euphemisms, instead of saying just plain "killed" or perhaps "slaughtered.") Anyway, she called the veterinarian who said:

"Look, I've killed twenty-one healthy young dogs this afternoon, but I am not going to do this big white-and-brown male in. How do you kill a dog that smiles at you every time you come near him with a syringe?"

And that really is how Sirius came to live on and to eventually join us here on the farm. The committee member went and collected Sirius and in a matter of days he was brought to Maryland where we met while I was doing the second of two television reports on the tragic fate of track greyhounds. He walked over to me. He looked up into my face and he smiled. That was it. How can you say no to a dog that is smiling at you? You can't. I couldn't, not any more than the veterinarian up there in New Hampshire could. Sirius asked the veterinarian for life, for a pardon, and he asked me for a home. He got both. I mentioned earlier, you may recall, that Yankee, the great bloodhound of so many years ago, and Brigitte, the toy poodle, were two of the three greatest dogs in my dog-enriched life. Sirius is the third.

What lesson does Sirius of the white teeth and pink gums teach us? If neither the New Hampshire veterinarian nor I could refuse Sirius his request for life because he smiled at us, how could the man who stuns the steer in the slaughterhouse raise his weapon while trying to avoid the animal's eyes if he truly believed that cattle think and feel emotions that he could even come close to relating to?

Once upon a time, and it wasn't all that long ago, very nearly one hundred percent of the people on earth depended to some degree on hunting to provide at least a part of their food on a regular basis. Hunting was an essential economic activity. Today fewer than one percent of the earth's inhabitants rely on hunting at all unless you want to include gunsmiths, dealers in four-wheel-drive vehicles, decoy carvers, and motel owners.

The line from 99.9 percent to 1 percent on a graph is a pretty convincing one. There have been some changes made. Obviously, land-use patterns, urbanization, big-business ranching, the convenience of retail outlets for all of our food requirements, refrigeration, vanishing habitat, changing moral values, all of these factors and a great many more have cut down on the extent to which man can and does hunt. But, even today, people who want to hunt still do. However, with the increasing awareness of the probable capacities of animals to think and feel, there appears to be even greater shrinkage in the hunting fraternity. People are doing other things with their discretionary time and money.

Because of the kind of life I live and the kind of places I go I meet an awful lot of people who hunt or used to hunt. I have known only a very few people in my life who didn't hunt and who then grew into hunters as they matured. On the other hand I have known scores of people who used to hunt, but who grew out of the practice. In my conversations with them they gave many reasons why they now carry a camera or binoculars instead of a bow, rifle or shotgun, and those explanations always seemed to include a changing view of animals. It is usually summed up with a non-committal

"Yeah, well, I just felt like I didn't want to do that anymore."

In short, I think that when even twenty percent of the world looked on hunting as necessary, and when slaughterhouses were nightmare places where fully conscious animals were hoisted bawling into the air by a chain around one leg to have their throats slit and be left to bleed to death, it really was necessary that animals not be perceived as thinking, feeling creatures. That is what has changed. The very suggestion of animal cognition has taken away the concealed places where less caring men and women used to hide from one of the most uncomfortable, nay intolerable of all human emotions, guilt.

9

I T IS BECOMING less and less difficult for us to deal with the idea of our dogs thinking and feeling. We are coming to that. More and more scientists, while short on details and real understanding, are moving in that direction, too. That is where the sun seems to be shining, where there is a break in the clouds. Now, what might dogs think about and how intelligent might they be? We can no more provide firm answers to those questions than we can the others. But we can think about them.

Furthermore, we should not get hung up on the subject of linguistics and perhaps this can be the last time I will have to protest. From here on we will refer to the dog as thinking. I am not going to ask the typesetter to put that word in italics every time it appears or clutter up the page by surrounding it with quotation marks. We are using the word by default because English, Albanian, Xosa, Tagalog, Basque, and the other tongues we are all familiar with fail us. I don't know what else to call cognition in animals, so we will say, acknowledging that it can possibly give the wrong impression if left unqualified, that dogs think. So be it. We have more important things to involve our attention.

Nature is pretty economical when it comes to directing energy in her plants and animals. Each species must evolve to be perfectly adapted to what is available. Imperfection is followed quickly by extinction. One form of imperfection would be misdirected energy and for a wolf in the wild and its recent descendant now on our hearth wool-gathering (figurative wool) would certainly be misdirected energy.

Until we know much more about cognition, ours or anyone else's, we can assume (NOT assert) that man may be the only species with the meandering intellect of a full-time thinker. On the basis of evolutionary tracks as well as observed behavior it would seem apparent that if species lower down the scale than man also deal with non-survival abstracts those species would most likely be among the great apes, chimps, gorillas, and perhaps orangutans. A lot of people feel that whales and dolphins, the cetaceans, are right up there, too. I will admit the idea is pleasing, but there are precious little data to enlighten us at the moment.

It is probably true, then, that dogs don't think about art, the origin of the universe, or geopolitics. What we are likely to do here is think as much about what dogs don't think about as we do about what they do. I should think that thought processes in dogs would concentrate on matters of survival and comfort. Dogs, really, are as hedonistic as cats and I can give one example of when I think some of our dogs think and what they very well might think about.

Our three greyhounds are very catlike in their desire for luxury and comfort. (They don't seem to think of comfort as a luxury.) I think their enormous muscle bundles and the relatively light fat and muscle covering on their hips, spines, ribs and long legs make the *soft life* rather more important to them than it might be to many other breeds. In fact, we have renamed Reggie, our first greyhound and a lovely animal by anyone's standards, *le pomme de terre de lit,* which is approximately French for couch potato.

Jill and I like our creature comforts, too. We have a great

king-sized bed with a terrific mattress and lots of comforters and down pillows, all the good stuff, no less than we deserve. During the day the bed is covered with a sheet thrown over whatever bedspread or quilt is being used. The three greyhounds, usually with at least two or three cats, luxuriate on this vast expanse of available hedonism. They ask to go out several times a day, do some laps if the weather is to their liking, and come in and head for that great bed.

If we go into our room all three greyhounds look at us, follow our course as we move to the closet or a bureau. Whatever we do they watch and listen. The reason for their somewhat greater-than-usual interest is easy to understand. They are waiting for a signal they *know* will eventually come. Note the suggestion here that they *know* something will occur. Not their instincts talking to them, not their glands secreting informational hormones, their minds are attuned to something they expect, anticipate, watch and listen for, and know they must respond to.

What happens is off-time: *"Get off, guys, our turn."* I am a selfish brute and I don't like sharing my mattress, however large it might be, with a bunch of pushy animals. Greyhounds have legs like pile drivers. When they stretch out they can pin you to a headboard like a reminder note pinned to a cork bulletin board. Cats entwine themselves around your neck, form a halo on your pillow—they can get downright icky when they come in quantity. It is not that I don't love them, it is just that I didn't marry them.

The greyhounds are so attentive because what is likely to happen next will affect them in a very personal way. Sooner or later there are going to be the voice and hand signals that mean heartlessness has won the day yet again and they will have to make do with a fake sheepskin on top of a pile rug stretched over foam rubber padding. Life can be cruel even in a loving home. If there is such a thing as reincarnation I want to come back as a dog in our home.

The greyhounds know full well what to expect. They hear me on the stairs, they watch me as I come into the room. I just know (although that is not a scientific way of putting things) that they are actually wondering (thinking) about whether the off-you-guys signal is coming immediately or whether there will be a reprieve while I go shower or go into the adjacent sitting room to catch up on a few video cassettes I have brought home from the office. They just have to be thinking about whether or not they have to get off right away or a little later. If I say (remember, I talk to our animals), *"Relax, guys, not yet,"* their eyes close, in unison. If I say, *"That's it, you dogs, hit the rugs,"* they get off, slowly, being essentially biddable critters, but all the while looking as injured and put upon as possible. You don't have to be a Jewish (or Irish) mother to give good guilt.

That is an anecdote, I own, but one that is repeated every night I am home. Since luxuriant comfort is a survival necessity (ask any greyhound, or any Caras animal, for

that matter), getting put off the bed is something a dog
might very well want to think about. The chaos theory or
relativity might not be parts of their intellectual agenda,
but getting off the bed does come close to a survival matter
when you have bony legs.

There is an interesting paradox, I think, that has come
into being in the last forty years or so, a period during
which the computer exploded outward and upward from
a relatively useful but not really essential calculator to become one of the dominant devices and perhaps even forces
in our lives. Many businesses, most perhaps, are utterly
helpless today when their computers *go down*. Airlines,
banks, brokerage firms, retail operations, warehouses,
hospitals, social service agencies, motor vehicle bureaus,
police departments, people just stand around looking helpless (which they are rapidly becoming) when their computers fail them. They looked betrayed and speak of the
mute, darkened computer terminals in hushed tones. They
are like orphans, abandoned, abused by the worst of all
possible fates. They don't remember how to do the things
that minor clerks did handily just three decades ago. And
anyway the data they need are hidden from them. What
is more inscrutable than a blank computer screen?

The paradox comes when scientists are more readily able
to ascribe mental (not electrical) activity to computers than
to living animals. It is the HAL 9000 syndrome. I had the
pleasure of working on the film *2001: A Space Odyssey*
with Stanley Kubrick and Arthur C. Clarke for several
years back in the mid-sixties and I am certain that many
of the scientists who dropped in at the MGM studios in
Borehamwood in Hertsfordshire north of London or who
were consulted during the research phase or production of
that remarkable film were far more comfortable with the
idea of HAL having a nervous breakdown than they would
have been with the concept that their dogs loved or feared
them, or were sad at anything above the glandular level.
That is strange if you think about it.

Dr. Ronald R. Griffin, who wrote the book *Animal Thinking,* published by Harvard University Press, has been a professor at Rockefeller University and has impeccable credentials. He simply can't be written off as some pie-in-the-sky sentimental dreamer. Having attended one conference where he was fairly deified, I can tell you he is a scientist's scientist. He had this to say: *"Many comparative psychologists seem almost literally petrified by the notion of animal consciousness."*

Petrified by animal consciousness, but not bothered a bit by a *computer* that says *"David, I'm afraid."* That has to be weird.

As indicated earlier, I do believe that we have needed animals to be witless bundles of glandular reactions so we could do to and with them the things we have historically been guilty of. It was bad enough that they bled (like us), but if they thought and felt in any way analogous to our own activities in that corner of the room it would be unbearable, *we* would be unbearable. Well, I believe they *do* have analogous activities, and along with a great many other people I believe we are pretty close to unbearable!

A few years back the Massachusetts Society for the Prevention of Cruelty to Animals changed the name of their colorful and informative magazine from *Our Dumb Animals* to *Our Animals.* The word *dumb* had been used historically in the sense of "without voices," not in the sense of without intelligence, but it carried an intolerable and outmoded connotation that just didn't fit our growing awareness that we have not really cornered the market in consciousness and emotions after all.

The idea that computers may eventually be complex enough to cross some invisible and certainly as yet ill-defined barrier and start to think and feel cannot be dismissed out of hand. A great many writers have speculated on the subject and volumes have been written. It is not the kind of thing I would be likely to illuminate with further discussion. That will have to remain for other peo-

ple to consider at length, however. But it certainly makes
for some exciting fiction.

I now live with just three computers and I have owned
only one other, but the dogs of my days probably come
close to fifty. I am much more comfortable talking about
dogs. I have had more opportunities to watch them and
make notes about them under many more varied circumstances. Besides, when I visit friends I inevitably pet their
dogs and ignore their computers. Except for the occasional
outburst of unquotable expletives, I never talk to my
computer. I just poke it. That is how this book is coming
into being. I am poking it up from my notes and diaries.
I don't give a fig how this machine feels about what I am
saying. I would, on the other hand, be truly concerned if
Duncan here at my feet were unhappy, *Wouldn't I, old
buddy?*

(This is very spooky. Immediately after I finished the
previous paragraph I decided to take a break and check on
the horses. I asked this computer to save what I had written
so far on a hard disc after repaginating. It refused. It started
to repaginate, but stopped on page 5 and wouldn't move.
This &$#$% thing is being spiteful! Do you suppose it is
related to HAL? I am not going to apologize to it. Duncan
and I are going across the way to see to the horses.)

We're back. Note one thing about the anecdotes we have
referred to so far. With one exception they are unexcep-
tional. That one is, of course, Angie and her friend and
nurse Sheba. That is so far beyond anything I have experienced that I can't even start to evaluate it. As for the
others, any observant dog owner could report their equal.
You just have to watch and listen.

By the time of the first World War animal behaviorists had
pretty much convinced themselves that there could be no
way to separate automatic, unthinking responses on the
part of animals to their environment from responses involving conscious choice. And that, with all good inten-

Dog teams pulling wheeled stretchers with the Red Army medical corps, World War II.

tions, became the truth the world of man lived by. Animals could not think. That knowledge came from on high and few dared question it except a few score million dog owners around the world.

It was, in retrospect, specious thinking on the part of science. What we were really saying was, we can't think of a way to sort this out, so therefore animals cannot think. Period. And that was acknowledged as scientific fact, based not on research but convenience. It was one of the laziest things science ever did. It bore the badge of orthodoxy so intensely that it literally kept most scientists from questioning it. After all, if you are going to try for tenure, or a chair at a good school, or want to be department chairperson in a school or museum, or are going to apply for a grant, stay cool, play it safe, don't challenge orthodoxy, don't make waves. They don't give medals for bravery under thought.

As I've mentioned, things have changed. Ethology, the study of the evolution of behavior, and psychology have both come a long way. What was true, what was scientific fact, is no longer clothed in such bulletproof armor. As a matter of fact, so many holes have been poked in that fabric of self-righteousness that the sun is pouring in and revealing it for the nonsense it has always been. It is now perfectly legal for dog lovers to say of their dogs what they have always known of their dogs. Dogs think, or whatever.

Let us first divide thinking into two modes. (We are still in a prescience stage here, hopefully asking intelligent questions so that they may one day be answered, intelligently.) There is thinking about incoming data from our sensory package and in both man and dog, we know, that package may have many more facets than we tend to allow it in our conventional appraisals. That mode is simply information processing and would represent thinking in its most rudimentary form. It reduces us all, man and animal alike, to soft tissue computers.

Thinking, however, almost certainly goes far beyond that and includes consciousness and knowledge, recall, decision making beyond the reflexive and is where plotting and planning would come in if and when it exists. That is where thinking really kicks into gear and gets going. Although we can't prove it, that is probably what is going on here as I think about what I think I have learned through my senses and on the basis of that write these words for your kind consideration. It is in that same mode that you read these words, deciding as you go to accept or reject what I suggest.

There is another little problem to get on the record. Although we do not really understand very much about thinking beyond data processing in ourselves we will still have no choice but to use ourselves as a base line. We have to deal with comparative cognition. Imperfect though our knowledge most certainly is, we know far more about what goes on in our own minds than we do about the comparable processes in dogs, elephants, whales, cats, chinchillas, wombats and gorillas.

Admittedly, we are using a virtual unknown, ourselves, as a control in the contemplation of a totally unknown phenomenon, animal cognition, but what other options are there for us to use? Literally, there are none. The choices available to us are vegetables (they probably don't think), minerals (I'd wager *they* don't think), other animal species (we know far less about them than we do ourselves, for the most part), nothing at all (we don't know how to do that very well), the animals under consideration themselves (that's how you draw a circle), or us, however faulty the process thereby becomes. Us it is, with apologies.

For a long time it was somehow assumed (but hardly proven) that conscious thinking was attendant only on learned behavior and that genetically programmed behavior—instinct—never had to involve a cognitive process. That is apparently not so. That means, in this expanded context, if a dog/wolf is startled by the blast of the air horn of an eighteen-wheeler roaring past on the highway he may jump by reflex. In fact, he had better. His genes should signal him to jump out of the way of danger without stopping to think about it because pausing to make it an intellectual process could prove to be a fatal error. He is designed that way just as we are. Avoidance of clear and present danger on a second-by-second basis is probably pretty much on automatic mode in all vertebrate animals at least and, we know, in many invertebrates as well. But that doesn't mean the startled dog can't ask himself a split second later, *"What the hell was that?"*

And how is this kind of consideration treated by our educational system even today? Again to quote Dr. Donald R. Griffin, who observes in the preface to the aforementioned book: *"Throughout our educational system students are*

taught that it is unscientific to ask what an animal thinks or feels.
Such questions are actively discouraged, ridiculed, and treated
with open hostility."

Those words were published in 1984. So we have the
strange paradox that while advanced thinkers and investigators are actively pursuing knowledge about how animals think and what they think, and writing scientific
papers on the subject, a very junior student who even asks
if animals think will have a probably very junior instructor
in high school or undergraduate college climb all over him
for daring to be so confrontational, to even wonder if
animals do such outrageous, disquieting things. Information, ideas, knowledge filters down slowly. Wisdom,
unfortunately, manifests itself in our educational systems
as a trickle, not a torrent.

As this book is being written the subject of communication among bees is being debated. During the 1960s Karl
von Frisch postulated that bees return to their hives when
they have discovered a good food source and do a ritualized
dance that enables the other bees to go directly to the source
and gather the nectar.

But von Frisch may not have discovered that at all. A
few researchers have recently suggested that although it is
demonstrable that bees return to their hives and do an
intricate dance after discovering food it may not be as much
communication as something else (the something else not
yet being satisfactorily defined). Despite the unfortunate
reaction to their heresy, they are trying to sort it out.

The amazing thing is that some scientists take all of this
very personally. Some behaviorists are not talking to other
behaviorists and the "offending" scientists may have actually placed their careers in jeopardy. Redefining truth
can be dangerous work when you can get it. There are less
hazardous occupations, like being a test pilot or putting
out oil well fires in Kuwait.

This kind of behavior by behaviorists has made natu-
ralists in the field and in the laboratory so afraid for their

own reputations they are often reluctant to report observations that suggest cognition on the part of the animals
they are studying. That probably keeps some badly needed
pieces of the puzzle from being available. We here shall be
made of stouter stuff. We shall fear not, neither shall we
deny what happens before our eyes.

An aside, because it shows how this kind of thing can
work. One animal you do not expect to see in Africa, no
matter how often you are there or for how long, is a black
leopard. The melanistic phase of the common everyday
spotted leopard, which is what a black leopard or panther
is, is fairly common on the Malay Peninsula, occasionally
seen in forested portions of India, but only rarely in Africa.
Being black can be an advantage in a dense forest, but it
is of no advantage at all and probably a deficit in savanna
country. Sun-dried grass can make a black cat stand out
and interfere with its ability to stalk prey. It is different
where there are dense stands of trees with shadows.

I had seen one black leopard in the wild, in Sri Lanka.
I had not expected to ever see one at all and was delighted
to have had the experience. I certainly didn't expect to see
another. Then, at ten o'clock one very sunny morning, on
the open savanna of the Mara Maasai in southern Kenya,
a very large and very black leopard ran across the open
ground between two ditches no more than a hundred feet
in front of me. There was no possibility of error. There it
was and there I was and I could have hit it with a stone.
I immediately decided that I would say nothing about it
and I cautioned the driver to adopt the same defensive
posture. There was nothing to be gained by having people
look at me with pity in their eyes. *"Poor boy has lost it,"* I
could hear them say. There is so much nature faking and
so many false claims for some sort of glory, I guess, that
it has come to that.

I only abandoned my resolve when a number of reports
began coming in about a black leopard being seen in the
Mara, in the general area where I had seen what was surely

the same animal. Finally, a member of the Kenyan game department asked me at a cocktail reception in Nairobi if I had heard anything about a black leopard when I was down in the Mara. I confessed, but I wouldn't have if there hadn't been the support of other observers, a fair number of them, immediately available. I think that that is what has happened in the field of animal cognition. *"Why should I put my head on the chopping block?"*

I have told this story before, but that was in another book long ago and it is worth repeating because I think it is illustrative if not remarkable. (Personally, I think it is remarkable, but that is subjective.) Yankee, our son's first bloodhound, was a splendid creature when he came on board at five months and became only more splendid with time. He was a great champion.

Top dog on our turf at the time was a five-year-old golden retriever named Jeremy Boob. He was as sweet and easygoing as the best examples of that wonderful breed can be, but he was a male albeit altered and he was mature and he had been first on the turf. As a male puppy Yankee would have to mind his manners. Yankee did. His genes if not his wits told him exactly how to behave toward Jeremy, acknowledging him as the Alpha dog.

Everything slipped easily into place. We always put Jeremy's dish down about fifteen seconds before Yankee was served. We did all of the reassuring things that kept Jeremy's nose from getting too far out of joint. The other dogs of the household, purebred and random-bred, happened to be bitches, so everybody had a comfortable, secure place.

Anyone who has had a retriever, golden or otherwise, knows how important it is for them to be given an opportunity to retrieve. It is not just a game with them, although it is assuredly that as well. It is an absolute compulsion. That is one place where their genes really come into their own. Retrievers fairly pulse with their built-in imperative. A retriever not given an opportunity to re-

trieve is like a border collie not given an opportunity to herd. He is an unfulfilled dog and probably a pain in the neck with the substitute activities he will have to invent to drain off his genetically propelled energies. If nothing else, retrievers should be asked to carry the newspaper inside, carry the mail down the drive from the mailbox, carry slippers from room to room. They should be given a chance to be themselves.

Yankee, away from his mother and littermates, soon forgot that he was a scent hound boasting an awesome capacity all of his own. He wanted to be like his new big-dog role model, Jeremy. He wanted to retrieve, too. Retrieving means being able to calculate a trajectory by sight. Throw a stick, ball or Frisbee, it doesn't matter what the projectile is, and the retriever sees it as a duck. If it is over land the retriever is virtually always there to catch it when it comes down. He knows exactly where it is going to

land. It is a wonderful skill to watch as it is being used. I
don't know that anyone understands how retrievers do it,
but millions of people have witnessed it.

So Yankee would dash off with the rest of the dogs
when the ball or stick became airborne, but he would
never, ever be at the point of impact. Jeremy won one
hundred percent of the time. Yankee, poor dear, with a
wonderful nose but unimpressive eyesight, would gallop
after the others, unable to understand that he had neither
the eyes nor the software to calculate a trajectory's rate of
decay. Still, he apparently thought of himself as a retriever
who would be like Jeremy some vague day in the future
when he grew up. In his heart of hearts he just knew that
one day he would be there first. While the crowds would
roar their approval, Yankee would snatch the missile from
the sky and dash home with the bacon, leaving Jeremy and
the other dogs behind thoroughly bewildered. Yankee
never lost faith. He thundered on with the rest of them,
waiting for his manifest destiny to manifest itself. Well, in
those endless retrieving trial forays on the beach behind
our house Yankee left a lot of footprints in the sand, but
none in the annals of retrieverdom.

But Yankee did grow up, that he managed to do. Jeremy
weighed about seventy pounds at his maturity, while Yankee, after his kind, came to weigh one hundred and thirty-
two pounds. With the attainment of adult size came a new
level of self-esteem for the bloodhound. Jeremy was Alpha
dog in most things, but now only by Yankee's sufferance.
Fortunately they were both very nice dogs, good friends
actually, and nothing really serious ever came to the test.
It would have been a terrible day for us all if it had. Our
lifestyle, then as now, depended on a sense of pack, family,
with the attendant good manners required by such a social
structure. There is no room for a fiery temper or a rotten
disposition.

Yankee, however, did finally figure out the key to the
retrieving game. Jeremy would still win every throw, Yan-

kee had apparently learned to live with that, but there was the matter of bringing home the bacon. Jeremy was still getting petted and thanked for bringing the projectile back to home base. Yankee learned to wait while Jeremy got the stick and then he would plant himself firmly between Jeremy and us, the place of the reward. He learned that sheer mass could stand for something in this world. In time it became impossible for Jeremy to get past the great hulk of a bloodhound. Jeremy did all of the work, but Yankee brought home the prize. We wondered if there would be yet another stage in this canine battle of wits. Could Jeremy beat that rap? Could he regain the crown that was by rights his very own? He could and he did in a most unexpected, but really in a most natural, way.

I don't know how it actually started, although I doubt that Jeremy cut the plan from whole cloth. One day Jeremy had to urinate—after he caught the stick, but before he brought it to us. That seems the most likely scenario. Nothing more exotic or arcane than that. Well, after all, both Jeremy and Yankee were males and Yankee had to do exactly what he was programmed to do at birth as a male of the species. He answered Jeremy's message by peeing on the same bush where Jeremy had just peed. Male dogs urinate very often as a territorial sign-posting ritual and other male dogs, detecting pheromones, communication chemicals, respond by doing the same thing in the same place. In a sense, the second dog and all subsequent ones are saying, *"Oh, yeah? Says who?"* But everybody seems to be good-natured about it. Contrast that with the behavior of female dogs. They just empty their bladders when they have to and get on with other things. Urinating isn't a way of life for them.

In that moment Jeremy shot for home with the prize while Yankee, preoccupied with his genetic compulsion, looked on helplessly. He really did look quite silly standing there on three legs with an expression on his face that seemed to say, *"Hey, wait for me."*

That was it, the die was cast. Jeremy saw the wonders he had wrought and from then on that was the way the game was played. Run, snatch the stick from the air, cock the old hind leg and streak for home and get all the praise. Never mind about old Yankee the hulk. He was no threat as long as his genes commanded him to do what wolves and dogs had been doing for eons. Yankee, for his part, never learned to beat the game.

Whenever I felt like taking time off from my labors and getting some air I would call out, "How would you guys like to . . ." I never got any further than that before I had dogs all over me. Jeremy, the most enthusiastic and capable retriever of all, was always the last to arrive. He had to stop at the water bowl first.

What was happening here? Jeremy did not do anything that was unnatural for a male dog and neither did Yankee, of course. But why was Jeremy doing it that way? Immediately after catching a flying stick and just before bringing the stick back for a reward—praise—knowing from experience that he would not be able to do the latter unless a huge hulk of a bloodhound was somehow distracted, he distracted the bloodhound. After watching the ritual enacted scores of times I have been tempted in weak moments to think of it as innovative behavior. But there are a lot of abstractions there if it were indeed actually innovative. (1) Jeremy would have had to understand that he had a problem. (2) He would have had to understand the real nature of his problem. (3) He would have had to realize there could be a solution. (4) He would have had to understand the kind of imperative Yankee would have to deal with if he, Jeremy, cocked his leg. That last part is very difficult to believe. Surely, using pheromones in urine to stake a claim is part of an instinctive package and not something a dog or wolf has ever had to intellectualize. But there would have had to have been further dealings with abstractions if Jeremy was truly innovating behavior. At some point he would have had to "say" to himself, *"Hey, if I do this, Yankee will have to do that, and then I will be able to do this, which will then solve that."* If Jeremy could deal with that many *if*s and with cause and effect to that degree, he could have played chess. And I am reasonably sure he couldn't even play Chinese checkers.

No, I don't really suggest that Jeremy figured out what to do in order to get an effect that would then let him do something else. Somehow, though, and this is undeniable because I did watch it go on for years, Jeremy did learn, perhaps it was serendipitous, but he did learn to behave in a certain way perfectly natural to him and get a desired result. I doubt that he figured it out, laid out a course of action, but he was obviously intelligent enough to realize that something he did made his life take a desirable turn. He kept doing it whenever the course of events brought him to that same point. It worked to his benefit, however it came to be first attempted, so he stayed with it.

Is any of this interpretation writ in stone? Heavens, no. It is simply how I interpret what I saw. I had no scientific protocol to guide me, no control groups for comparison, nothing that could even resemble scientific methodology. I cannot, however, understand at all how Sheba—remember Sheba and Angie?—how that wonderful little dog did what she did, either. The point is, Sheba did it and Jeremy did his thing and it is very difficult to believe either enacted his or her whole scenario without something more profound than genetic material, i.e., instincts, or glandular secretions.

Jeremy urinating, Sheba cuddling and staying tight with her pack, these were natural ways for them to behave up to a point. They didn't really have to learn to do anything new, just what to do of the many things they already knew how to do and when to do those things, and in what sequence triggered by what impulse, in response to what outside signal. If either dog had been faced with unnatural acts, striking a match, depressing a clutch pedal, operating a zipper, something with no analog in the dog's normal life, they would have had to be trained, and it is amazing how much training a dog can accept once his (or her) trainer has his (or her) pupil's attention.

Mike, father to our border collie Duncan, the famous movie star dog, had a very challenging scene in *Down and*

Out in Beverly Hills. He is offered a can of dog food. Clint Rowe, a remarkable trainer, surely one of the best, taught Mike to (1) approach the food, (2) sniff it, but not taste it, (3) look at the actress playing the maid, (4) bark, (5) pick up the container of food, (6) carry it to a pedal-operated kitchen garbage pail, (7) step on the pedal, (8) drop the container into the pail, (9) release the pedal and (10) walk out of the room. He had to do all of that without looking at Clint who was stationed nearby. Mike had to follow the sequence in that order, he had to understand somehow that stepping on the pedal opened the garbage can because he had to step on it hard enough to get the pail to open wide enough for him to drop the food container in, and he very well may have picked up on the fact that lifting his foot off the pedal allowed (caused) the container to close. Approaching the food and sniffing it were natural

Munito, a mathematical dog, Paris, nineteenth century.

to Mike. Barking is natural, too, but not necessarily in that context. Probably not, in fact. The rest of the action Mike was called upon to perform was unnatural and had to be learned as new skills, based on nothing really very useful to dogs. When a dog like Mike is responding to an owner-trainer like Clint Rowe, the dog inevitably wants to learn. That is an end in itself and so is the praise that always follows a successful mission. There is absolutely no end to a dog's capacity to soak up praise. What interests us here is that even in a sequence as complex as the one described for Mike, the dog is able as well as willing to learn. But that may still not be abstract thinking.

The dogs we live with, and this is also true of all of the higher wild animals as well, at least, and our domestic livestock, they all have to come to sensible solutions so many times every day in order to coordinate their behavior that it is difficult to see how they could possibly do what they do without thinking in some way or other. A case at hand this moment:

Vicki Croke, an outstanding feature writer for the Boston *Globe* who went on safari with us in East Africa, has arrived for the weekend. She called and asked if she could bring her dog, Lacy, an Irish wolfhound, with her. She hates to put Lacy into a kennel any more often than she absolutely must. And Lacy hates being kenneled in a strange environment. Most dogs do. Obviously, we said yes, in fact we said that she couldn't come without her dog.

The Irish wolfhound is the tallest although not the heaviest of all dog breeds. They are true giants and Lacy is no exception. Obviously, when Vicki and her gargantuan dog arrived there was a lot of sizing up that had to go on. That is pro forma. We do the same thing when a new face is introduced in the workplace or playground. We go so far as to appoint committees to do it for us in the condominium and country club settings.

Lacy had had no experience whatsoever with cats and

had to be told that cats are interesting to watch and smell, but they are not for chasing or munching on. Lacy has settled down to watch the cats and the cats, after the initial shock of finding a horse-sized dog in their kitchen, have settled down to watch Lacy. The cats walk right under her nose.

All of the dogs had to evaluate the new event, too. They love new things happening on the farm because it apparently gives them something fresh to *think* about. Lacy had to work out an instant relationship with each dog and each dog obviously had to undertake the same procedure.

One of the first things Lacy did when she came in was hit the old water dish. She had, after all, arrived in a car and cars make dogs thirsty. The Thistle Hill dogs and cats gathered at a respectful distance and watched. They literally sat around in a semicircle and watched Lacy drink as if she had invented some fabulous new way of splitting the atom.

"Imagine that," the Thistle Hill crowd seemed to say, *"she drinks, just like us."* Or, perhaps, *"Well, she drinks like us despite her absurd size so she can't be all that bad."*

I am not trying to emulate the great Richard Adams. This isn't *Watership Down,* but the undeniable fact is that the animals all found Lacy fascinating, she found them at least as interesting, and now, a few hours later, everybody is settled in and nary a feather nor a blade of fur has bristled.

Are we to believe that all of this accommodation by all concerned, all of this evaluation of possible danger (an Irish wolfhound can look dangerous) has gone on and all of the individual peaces have been made without any cognitive process at all? I cannot believe that. I see no compelling reason to try.

One brief side observation: many really strict, dyed-in-the-wool, think-my-way-or-I'll-kill-you, orthodox behaviorists disregard subjective feelings and conscious thought in human beings as well as in animals. So the people who would tend to most staunchly oppose what

we are saying here would also tend not to believe that you
and I can think about these things or have subjective feelings either. One thing has always puzzled me about that.
Since those extreme behaviorists (they live in Skinner
boxes, I am sure) are presumably human beings, too, however misguided we may think they are, what glands do
you suppose they use in order to decide that we are all just
a mess of glands and genetically programmed responses?
How do they get to think that we can't think or feel or
that animals can't? And if we argue with them and they
get angry, I have seen them do that, angry and disdainful,
what glands do they have to store anger and disdain in
when they aren't using them? I think they are quite silly.

Toward the end of the nineteenth century, in 1894 I believe
it was, a scientist by the name of C. Lloyd Morgan created
what was to become known as Morgan's Law of Parsi-
mony. It stated: *In no case may we interpret an action as the
outcome of the exercise of higher psychical faculty, if it can be
interpreted as the exercise of one which stands lower on the psy-
chological scale."*
   Sounds good to me. If you pick up a hot frying pan
with a metal handle and drop it, why suggest you think
very fast when we know darn well that you didn't even
think about how hot the handle was until well after you
had let go of it? What Morgan was trying to do was create
some kind of order out of what was and still is largely
chaos. Like Darwin, Morgan believed in the evolution of
mental abilities.
   If you think of the animate world as consisting only of
mammals, then we are vastly different from our dogs. Two
legs as opposed to four, roughly two months of pregnancy
as opposed to nine, a verbal language that can deal with
incredible abstractions, art and aesthetics with no visible
counterparts, nothing but a whole long string of enormous
differences.
   But the livng world is not just mammals. Hardly. It is

made up of a great array of life forms that push all of us mammals much closer together when the whole picture is taken into account. We have in common with our dogs warm blood, a four-chambered heart, we give birth to living young, we care for our young, and that is a major imperative in much of what we do. We both communicate with each other by sound and posture. We have complex social structures, we are physically symmetrical, we are at times aggressive toward our own kind. Even more telling, we have central nervous systems composed of neurons which are connected by synapses. We are connected in thousands of ways by our evolutionary track up out of the primeval slime, so why would we have gone off in different directions when it comes to cognition, thinking? What is there to suggest that we in fact did any such thing?

Dogs and their ancestors, like human beings and our ancestors, faced then and face now a world full of challenges ranging from mate attracting or claiming and infant rearing to food getting and protecting. We both need some kind of shelter at various phases of our lives (a female with cubs, for example), we both have dangers to avoid. In some cases, like cave bears and rattlesnakes, the dangers have been exactly the same during our evolution.

Demonstrably, the best device for handling all of these complex elements of existence is intelligence, thinking. It works so well we have been steadily evolving the capacity in our species, and I know of not a single shred of evidence that would demonstrate that dogs haven't been doing the same thing, albeit at a different rate, in different ways, to different levels to solve sometimes, but only sometimes, different problems.

Awareness of self and what self is doing while it is doing it (or perhaps just remembering it as recent activity) would almost certainly go along with thinking at almost any level. We can almost state with certainty that if an animal is aware of its actions, it is aware of itself. And if it is aware of itself, it is involved in some kind of thinking or, as our scientific friends would say, some level of a cognitive process.

Oomiac, the Siberian husky, bless her, was a thief. Lots of dogs are. It is perfectly natural for dogs to take what they want when they want it and when it is available. It can take a lot of negative reinforcement to train that out of them. With some dogs it just doesn't take hold. Oomiac was such a dog. But Oomiac, like most canine thieves, made stealing an art. She waited until you were out of the room. She stopped whatever evil things she was doing if she heard you coming, she tried to look uninvolved and did everything but buff her toenails and let the cats take the blame if you blocked her route of escape. She sank into despair, wore a look of abject misery if caught in the act. I don't believe it is possible to say that she wasn't aware of what she was doing. She hung around looking disinterested until the coast was clear—which means to me she

was planning her misdeeds. She knew what she was doing, who she was, and whether or not it was worth it to her to risk being caught and taking all of the ensuing static and disapproval. I wouldn't be surprised to learn that she thought about the consequences of her life of potential misadventure more than a lot of drug addicts and criminals do today.

It is interesting to me that one of the reasons some people have given for not believing animals think is that they don't believe animals can look ahead and deal with probable consequences, that animals are so very existentialist. That is to say, they can't or at least don't take the future into account the way sixteen-year-olds do when they drop out of high school, the way alcoholics and other substance abusers do when they give in to an urge to escape, to fly free of responsibility, the way people do who expose themselves to unwanted pregnancies (viewed from either parent's perspective) or to AIDS. Apparently, if we were to believe the unbelievers, people can see ahead but very often don't, while dogs can't see ahead but very often do. I am sure that makes sense to someone.

I don't really mean to be snide and I don't suggest that dogs can think about what they would like to be when they grow up (a fool's errand in their case, since they don't grow up), but they are aware, I believe, of themselves and what they are doing and how those actions are going to go over with the pack. In a word, they think.

Dogs, like people, must be shaped to a marked degree by their surroundings and a true test of their intelligence would be their efforts to shape those surroundings. Yankee did that. He was more than manipulative with us, although he was certainly that—most dogs do most of their environment shaping by manipulating the human members of the pack—he ran a tight ship. He liked things to be his way, dignified, quiet and orderly, and he hated any kind of an unseemly row. Decorum, I think, is the right word. He liked things to be decorous.

His daughter was Penny, a lovely bloodhound who had a great start for a spectacular show career until illness grounded her for life by requiring that she be spayed. When she was about eight months old and very, very full of herself, she showed one moment of ill temper that she regretted for hours afterward. My mother-in-law was feeding the dogs that particular morning and had fed Yankee in one corner of the kitchen and put Penny's food down in another. She changed her mind for some reason and went to move Penny's bowl to another spot and Penny reacted to the move toward her dish with a ferocious and really quite convincing growl. I doubt that she would have really bitten or even snapped, but we were never to find out.

Yankee literally hurtled across the room like a bulldozer. His body slammed poor, startled Penny into the refrigerator door, nearly knocking her out. She slid to the floor and it took her nearly a minute to shake herself free of the shock and try to stand. A hundred and thirty pounds of dog playing missile can be shocking. Yankee stood there looking at her—if he had been built right I am sure he would have put his hands on his hips—and Penny sat down looking very hangdog. A minute or so later Yankee was back at his dish and Penny, very slowly and quietly, went back to hers. Yankee had made his point. He just wasn't having it, not in his house, not on his watch. Penny was never heard to growl at a person again, not in her long and pleasant life.

There was another occasion. A bloodhound puppy we had visiting us was playing the hoydenish puppy role to the hilt dashing from room to room, just being generally busy and noisy. Yankee was trying to sleep in the dining room and rolled his eyes back and forth watching the miniature image of himself hurtling past, again and again. He moved only his eyes and eyebrows while all of this racket was going on around him.

Like the true bloodhound he was, Yankee had enormous

ears. They spread on either side of his head like scatter
rugs as the puppy gyrated around him. There was one false
step. The poor puppy ran across one of Yankee's ears as
if it really was a rug and that was it for Yankee. With a
mighty roar he was off the floor and slammed the puppy
on the top of her head with a forepaw, mushing her face
to the floor. You could hear her teeth smashing into the

floor, in fact, and the poor little thing whimpered as she made her way as far away from Yankee as she could get. The big old guy lay back down and closed his eyes, certain that his nap would not be interrupted again. Yankee did indeed run a tight ship.

From a naturalist's point of view we could ask why wouldn't the forces that gave dogs cognition as a survival tool have given the same device to, let us say, codfish? We don't know, of course, that codfish don't think about all kinds of submarine matters, but there are clues to the big picture. Brain size is one, but the most telling is probably the number of offspring different species produce. It matters a great deal to nature (because of language limitations we have to personify myriad forces here and think in terms of "mother nature"—bear with it) whether an individual wolf makes it to maturity and is able to reproduce. Species survival, for nature, is what it really is all about. Canines reproduce relatively slowly, have a very limited number of young each time, and must struggle to teach their young how to survive while they are feeding and protecting them. Nature, on the other hand, doesn't have to worry about a codfish. One medium-sized female codfish—called a hen—will produce as many as ten million eggs in a single season. A really large specimen may produce two or three times as many, so there is that factor. For comparison, thousands of years ago, when there was plenty of room for wolves, this entire planet didn't produce one million wolf embryos a year, not nearly. Another thing, how many millions of their eggs reach maturity is of no concern at all to the codfish of either sex. They don't feed their young, protect them, or even know them. Codfish don't have to think to survive as a species. We do, and wolves/dogs do.

10

To see the foregoing discussion of our modern dog in a meaningful context, to gather it all together, we have to consider how our pet subject came into existence. It is an amazing story and it saw and was a response to the interplay of many forces. The dog we know did not pop into being at our feet or beside our favorite chairs, not quite. It is, however, a species that has come in from the cold, unfortunately too often into the fire of our disregard and our persistent overemphasis on dominion. It has been a saga, an adventure, and something of a miracle, or, perhaps more accurately, a series of miracles that we call evolution. To people who still get a tingling feeling when they hear the word *evolution,* I would suggest that evolution is nothing other than creation on a different time scale. There is nothing more miraculous than evolution/continuing creation, so I really can't imagine why it makes some people squirm.

No one said, specifically, *"Let there be dog."* The great miracle of another species being able to bond with us and fulfill, of all things, some of our emotional needs came about over millions of years of evolutionary experimentation, if you go to the roots, an enormous amount of trial and error without us even in mind. It seems we were on our own way up out of the primeval slime at the same time. Not all that long ago, as these things are reckoned, our paths crossed and a bargain with wondrous advantages for our species and some for the other was struck. And what a tale there is to tell.

We will have to get by in this chapter without much in the way of anecdotes, obviously, and we will have to allow

Chows of the Chinese Wei Dynasty (third century A.D.) and, center, a Spitz of the Han Dynasty (206 B.C.–A.D. 220).

that science takes many things for granted when it comes to frequently questionable evidence of fossil remains. All of the studies of prehistory that we will refer to and to large measure rely on must be viewed as work in progress. It almost certainly always will be ongoing, at least in the foreseeable future. There appears to be no other way. And being a part of the past is a situation that can never be corrected, as far as we know. We can move matter around even to the point of creating new elements and species (the dog is, after all, just such a new species), but we cannot shuffle time. More's the pity. Although we are blocked in our roles as witnesses by the realities of time, let's try to do some of that evolution watching in our own imaginations (which can be pretty satisfying if not exactly like seeing it firsthand).

The true history of the dog begins far, far back in that irretrievable warp of time. Ever since those first microscopic glimmerings in warm, shallow waters there was movement—sometimes slow, sometimes a little faster, in the general direction of the toy poodle, the greyhound and the beagle. It has been an inexorable force, just like the force behind the evolution of all living species, contemporary like our own and those sadly long gone. Species ride the point of their own spears as they are thrust on ahead. Without that force and that movement the species of plants and animals we know today wouldn't be here. For convenience, though, and for no other reason whatsoever, we will pick up on the remarkable journey of the dog on the point of its spear during the Age of Reptiles when the terrible lizards known as dinosaurs ruled the world. It is one of the most exciting periods in the history of life on earth, a suitably dramatic point to launch the saga of the dog.

In the Permian and Triassic periods, starting about two hundred and seventy-five million years ago (all of these "ago" numbers, usually in the tens or hundreds of millions of years, are of necessity likely to be approximations, you will understand) and extending over a period of perhaps fifty million years, a group of specialized dinosaurs known as synapsids arose and flourished. They replaced other reptiles, those surviving the universal geological cataclysms—most particularly the emerging continents.

Those reptiles had developed feathers and fur to replace their scales (some of which had long since evolved into huge bonelike plates). The dinosaurs opting for feathers would eventually vanish, but they would leave birds behind in their place. The ideas that constitute the bird were good ones, feathers and sustained flight and thermoregulation. Those reptiles evolving fur would also vanish and be replaced by another better evolutionary idea, mammals. That is where the synapsids figured in. They were for a time the most advanced of all the early paramammals or mammal-like reptiles. While all of the other changes in life-forms were occurring there was already a selection for larger brains, i.e., intelligence.

By the time the Mesozoic Era was in full bloom, perhaps two hundred and fifteen to two hundred and twenty million years ago, the synapsids had just about run their course on earth and had been supplanted by a group of reptiles known as the archosaurs. Just as the synapsids had risen to the top as the dominant forms of the earliest mammal-like dinosaurs by rising over the pelycosaurs between fifty and fifty-five million years earlier, they were now phased out themselves by new and improved models. The group that replaced them, the archosaurs, would eventually vanish, too, replaced by mammals.

The synapsids during their period of glory had ranged in size from that of a small newt to about the size of a hippopotamus. They had been able to take advantage of opportunities in a wide variety of habitats, far more than the other less-evolved dinosaurs had been able to manage. From that widely diverse group the mammals are believed to have come one slow step at a time, dropping off along the way into the pit of extinction many experiments that simply did not work out. Advancing intelligence, though, remained on the successful inside track.

The mammals, as they evolved, apparently had larger brains than any of the reptiles had ever had and for that reason, and others, they were far more adaptable. They not only had fur to protect them, but they had evolved the ability to minutely regulate their own body temperatures from inside themselves. We have long *assumed* that the dinosaurs did not have that ability, but we may have been wrong all along. Dinosaurs may in fact have been light years ahead of other reptiles in this regard.

The mammals, though, didn't have to spend their lives playing tag with the sun the way animals like snakes and turtles have to do right into the present time. That new freedom enabled them to explore habitats and lifestyles that perhaps had been closed to dinosaurs and certainly to the other reptiles that had evolved before the dinosaurs, coexisted with them, and would outlast them—things like the crocodilians.

As habitats evolved so did the plants and animals that had the versatility to adapt to them. The real conquest of virtually the entire planet had begun. The mammal idea was as inexorable as the geology of the planet itself. Once it started moving forward everything would eventually have to give way before it or find a way of fitting in without seriously challenging what have become known as the truly higher animals. (Actually, anything with a backbone can be described as a higher animal, but of the higher, mammals are surely the highest, thus far.)

The new mammals evolved into a vast array of often experimental forms (although many did fail, as it always is in the evolution of new species) as a result of their flexibility and perhaps in part because of their growing intelligence. All kinds of niches were probed, explored, and most of them eventually exploited for whatever they had to offer. The different lifestyles made different demands for intelligence, but that force continued to grow where and as it was needed.

The mammals worked on the same kind of time frame their antecedent dinosaurs had used, millions upon tens of millions of years. Wondrous though we mammals are, we started out slowly and only later picked up just a little steam. For it all, we are still pretty slow evolvers. That is just how these things work. Actually, since the only alternative to perfection is extinction, a desert pupfish, a cockroach, a scorpion, and a land crab have done just about as good a job as we have, but certainly the mammals have evolved the most diverse and elegant systems of all and gone the furthest. We can give them (ourselves included) that.

Moving right along, to the Tertiary Period, between thirty and sixty million years ago, was when the creodonts came into being and flourished. *Creodont* is somewhat of a catchall designation for a large group of animals that were spread around the world, everywhere it seems but Australia and South America. Many of them were not so closely connected in an evolutionary sense as they were linked by an idea. They were successful flesh-eaters and their lifestyle proved that the other mammals of the world could adjust their reproduction rate to accommodate predation. In fact, the success of the predators was dictated by their prey.

Predators that could most efficiently hunt with the lowest mortality rate among their own kind prospered when prey was available. That is reflected in today's world by the fact that in most ecosystems predators' populations are dictated by the prey base, more so than the other way around. Most people have that wrong.

Even very large animals with the rapid metabolism of predators could feed themselves without seriously impacting their prey's numbers. And smaller predators could also utilize birds, reptiles, some amphibians and fish—even

insects—in a variety of highly specialized lifestyles. All of
this kind of thing had worked for the predatory dinosaurs
and would work again with the far more intelligent mammals. That balance, an achievable equilibrium, opened the
way for the wolf and the cocker spaniel. As for the prey
animals, essentially hoofed species for just about all of the
larger predators, real intelligence was not anywhere near
the imperative it was for species that were forced to hunt
for a living. As someone once asked, rhetorically (I don't
remember who it was or where I read it, or else I would
give credit): *"How bright do you have to be to stalk a blade of
grass?"*

As intelligent as the creodonts may have been (when
compared with dinosaurs), they had to have been pretty
slow-witted for the main thrust of mammalian evolution.
In the Miocene Epoch (about seven million years ago) they
vanished, pushed aside because the development of their
brains was not keeping up with the competition. Failing
to do that has turned out to be fatal to a species. Either a
species gets out of the race in time and finds alternative,
less challenging ways to make a living, or it is bound to
be swamped.

About the same time the creodonts were rising up, probably from insect-eating animals of very small size, sixty
to sixty-five million years ago, a group that has lasted into
our time, the Carnivora, was moving onto center stage as
well. These were animals destined to be stars. They were
the competition. They were advanced flesh-eaters with carnassial teeth on the side that overlapped and cut flesh and
even bone like powerful scissors. They also had small,
sharp incisor teeth in front for holding prey and large, often
daggerlike canine teeth for delivering a lethal stab (they
still have that array). And even more important, they had
brains that showed great promise. Intelligence, not just
carnassial teeth, enabled the carnivora to crowd out the
creodonta, although it took them over fifty million years
to do it. The time scale was still not a snappy one

even if the eventual results were destined to be flashy and extremely successful.

Not all flesh-eating mammals today belong to the Order Carnivora. The very impressive orca or killer whale is truly carnivorous, totally so, but it is in no way related to Carnivora. Chimpanzees eat monkeys, baby antelope and anything else they can catch and handle, but they are certainly not members of the Order Carnivora even if they are part-time carnivores. Many of the Carnivora—pandas and most of the bears, for example—live for at least a part of each year on vegetable matter. Shrews are not Carnivora, but they are regular little hunting demons. Ask any mouse, vole, or mole. Carnivora are joined together in their order by tooth structure and other anatomical peculiarities, not by diet.

The ancestors of our modern Carnivora are even more confusing as a family than the creodonts had been. The family in retrospect is called Miacidae and to it has been assigned all kinds of predatory mammals that probably were not closely related at all. Many of them were undoubtedly small and weasel-like and lived in forests. They were probably largely tree-borne at first and their fossil record is somewhat disappointing, to say the least. When more fossils do eventually turn up and when the partial specimens already in museums are reevaluated, it is likely that Miacidae as a defensible single family will fail the test of careful scrutiny and a new predator's family tree will emerge from the mists. That kind of thing is *de rigueur* in paleontology and should not be seen as cause for derision. Quite to the contrary, it is a fact of ancient death. And it does show the probing, scientific vitality of paleontology.

However unstable or unverifiable a single family called Miacidae may eventually prove to be, most of our predatory mammals today apparently grew up out of "it." The cats, or Felidae; the weasels, or Mustelidae; the bears, or Ursidae; the hyenas, or Hyaenidae, the latter more like the cats than dogs; the raccoons and diverse kin or the Pro-

cyonidae (many scientists today place the giant panda in
with the raccoon kind); the mongooses and their kin or
Viverridae; and, of course, the canids or Canidae.

Up until four and a half or five million years ago there
was another family in the order Carnivora, the family Amphicyonidae, the so-called bear-dogs. They were an inter-

esting and varied group, actually, and spread out across Africa, Asia, Europe, and North America. They included the species that probably crowded the creodonts offstage. They tended to be bearlike in shape, even though some of them were apparently quite small, but their heads were definitely already getting very doglike and so were their teeth. Interestingly enough, they were flat-footed, "plantigrade," like the bears of today and very uncatlike in that. Cats are "digitigrade"—they walk on their toes and have the capacity for great speed available to them when they need it. Then, slightly before four million years ago, the Amphicyonidae were phased out and replaced by the Canidae, the dogs.

Now we are closing in on our main topic. The canines or Canidae had been coming on for thirty-five million years when they pushed aside the "bear-dogs." They were digitigrade, like the cats, which helped make them both swift and agile. They evolved in favor of long legs, incredible sight, hearing and smell, and certainly intelligence. That thread was still there, as it had been for scores of millions of years. Victory, as far as we know, always went to the more intelligent line of evolution.

The canines started to develop tight and complicated social bonds and were as agile mentally as they were becoming physically. (That next-to-the-last point is an assumption. Since behavior evolves, just as body forms do, we are giving the social behavior of the wolf/dog an early start. It would at least explain in part the success of Canidae.) The canids could adapt. They ate some vegetable matter when it was necessary and could live on carrion as well as their own kills. Because of their ability to coordinate group activity they could drive other animals, even quite large ones, off their kills and commandeer the prizes for themselves. Sharp senses, successful social groups, and especially brains were making the difference. The groundwork was being laid for our domestic dogs.

Those early canids tried all sorts of styles and techniques.

Some, like *Hesperocyon,* an animal shorter than three feet
from nose to tail, must have looked more like a very large
mongoose than a timber wolf, but he was a canid. Interestingly, the family Canidae appears to have evolved entirely in North America. No really early forms of Canidae
have ever been found anywhere else and at this point are
not likely to be. It could happen, of course, but it does
seem unlikely. At about the same time *Phlaocyon,* roughly
the same size as *Hesperocyon,* emerged in North America
looking more like a raccoon than a fox or coyote. Neither
form would survive into even recent times.

Probably one of the first members of the family Canidae
that we could have looked at, even at a distance, and recognized as a dog type was *Cynodesmus.* He was a bit over
three feet long and came into being roughly thirty million
years ago. He was about the size and general shape of a
large, modern coyote. His legs were definitely already doglike, but not quite yet evolved enough to allow him very
much in the way of speed or stamina as they are reckoned
today. He was, though, on the right track or at least pointing in the right direction. But by the early Miocene Epoch,
less than twenty-five million years ago, he was gone. Yet
another experiment had failed. Hundreds more were yet
to come.

Between four and five million years ago the dog group
staged a real spectacular in North America. There came
into being a number of wolflike species that grew to be
the size of modern grizzly bears. Gigantism wasn't a very
good evolutionary idea, apparently, not among predators,
because none survived. None of those monsters belonged
to the genus *Canis* that includes all of the wolves and dogs
alive today, not all of the canids, but all of the wolves and
their direct descendants.

We don't have a very clear and totally satisfying link for
today's genus *Canis* with the probably hundreds of earlier
failed canid evolutionary experiments, but a form called
Tomarctos is frequently given the credit for being the ances-

tor of today's wolf/dog, perhaps by default. By the time
the Pleistocene was here, roughly a million and a half years
ago—just yesterday in terms of the time frame we have
been using—*Canis dirus* was in Los Angeles, or at least in
what would eventually be Los Angeles. His kind were
dying in the La Brea tar pits by the thousands. This gigantic
wolf was between six and seven feet long. It could have
been an awesome hunter, but it also could have been more
of a scavenger. We are not certain which it was but that
latter supposition would explain why so many were trapped in the tar and sucked down to their deaths. As the
giant ground sloths, camels, and other incredible animals
of that time got trapped, the probably-not-yet terribly
bright dire wolves seemed to have jumped in on top of
them for a free feast—their last, as it turned out. It is
thought by many paleontologists that there were titanic
battles between dire wolves and sabre-toothed tigers, judging by the marks found on the fossilized bones of both
species. The fights were probably over prey. Now, *these*
would have been fights to see! And so close to where
Hollywood's cameras would eventually be!

The dire wolf didn't last, but the genus *Canis* did and
does today hold all of our dogs. And so it came to be.
Missing only the saga of domestication, that is the history
of the dog as we know it. Again, there was a constant
honing of many characteristics and physical skills. The legs
got better, the stance took the animals up onto their toes
and elongated their feet, the hind foot went from five to
four toes, breathing and body cooling modified to give the
animals greater stamina and impressive speed. But always
the animal was pointed in the general direction of intelligence. We don't know what kind of social life the dire
wolves had (their great size makes one suspect that they
did not go around in really large packs and still feed themselves), but behavior according to the science of ethology
is no less a product of evolution than body form, as we
have already noted. Wolves, *Canis,* evolved toward social

skills and that is what makes their descendants, our dogs, such totally satisfying pets. Not all intelligent animals are strongly social and not all very social animals are smart. Bees, ants, wasps, termites, at least some species of each, and naked mole rats as well, are highly social, but not awfully bright. Still, in wolves, social structure and intelligence seem to have grown apace.

Now for the next stage of our journey, domestication and what may yet come after that essential first phase in this fascinating and oh-so-satisfying relationship has passed.

11

In his early stages, it is often stated, man probably did not have many profound effects on his environment, although some of his hunting methods were wasteful and could have had a temporary effect on local populations of prey. It is also possible that he set but did not control fires and that presumably would have caused some deforestation, again locally, and perhaps even some desertification or at least erosion. The effects, however, were probably not profound, merely local, and almost certainly did not cause dramatic or long-lasting changes in weather patterns.

Our early ancestors were hunter-gatherers and everything they took was part of a renewable resource. Gathering fruits and nuts, shellfish, hunting small animals by running them down or later larger animals by running them off cliffs (very wasteful) was not that far removed from the things their far more apelike ancestors had had to do to earn their living.

We probably evolved rather rapidly into human beings because we added flesh to our diet and became hunters even more than gatherers. We could always fall back on vegetation when meat was in short supply, but when meat was there on the hoof we apparently went for it with gusto. There was the added incentive of pelts. A dead bison or wolf could warm us on the outside as well as the inside.

In these considerations keep in mind how very brief our time frame has become. When we spoke of dinosaurs, early mammal-like reptiles, and then the earlier carnivorous mammals, we used skips and leaps of tens of millions of years without embarrassment. We are now down to not very many tens of thousands of years. Virtually generations. We have been honest-to-goodness human beings for a mere eye blink's worth of history.

About ten thousand years ago man was far brighter than anything else on the planet. He was developing culture, probably art, organized hunting, tool-making in a wide variety of designs and to many ends, and he was well on his way to settlements, farms, villages and marketplaces. And sometime during the gap between ten and twenty-five thousand years ago he domesticated animals. It's probable that he started domesticating dogs twenty thousand years ago and was using them to herd animals only five thousand years later.

Of all the raw material that was handed to emerging man—flint, tubers, wood, skins, fire, wild forms of maize and rice and wheat—the wolf with the dog in its loins was one of the most promising and most precious. A nice fire can be restful and comforting on a cold evening, it is true, but the wolf/dog was a gift that gave something to man's psyche. The dog was to offer mental as well as physical health, although we are just beginning to understand that wild and wonderful phenomenon called bonding.

The gradual emergence of *Canis familiaris,* the domestic dog, from the genes of *Canis lupus,* in one subspecies or another (as we said earlier, it has been generally assumed that that subspecies was *C. l. pallipes*), was a series of events that is difficult to reconstruct. Guessing can be fun, though. An educated guess, after all, is just about a theory. There is evidence from a paleontological site called Zhoukoudian in northern China that an earlier version of us, *Homo erectus,* existed there at the same time as true wolves, *C. lupus.*

There is no way of knowing how they might have inter-
acted, but it is almost certain they would have. They were
both carnivores, although that early version of us did not,
of course, belong to Carnivora, and there was possibly
some recipredation (a word specially invented for this occasion, so don't try to look it up), i.e., given the chance,
one ate the other. That could have led to some mean-
spiritedness on the part of both animals. Not to worry,
they were to get over it. No problem, really, since old *H.
erectus* went extinct not long after that.

In the Chernigou region of the Ukraine, at a site known
as Mezin, remains have been found that are clearly pure
wolf; nearby are remains that appear to be canids well on
the way to becoming dogs. Some scholars conclude that
domestication was underway there. Those are finds from
the late Paleolithic, toward the end of the early Stone Age.

About ten thousand years ago a group of *Canis* skulls,
nearly thirty of them, got buried close together by unknown events near what is now Fairbanks, Alaska. It is
believed our kind of people were there at that time and
the muzzles on those canine skulls appear to be considerably shorter than those of wolves found in Alaska today.
(I once went fishing in a river east of Kotzebue with some
Eskimos. The place is known as Onion Portage and digs
there have shown the site to have been in use as a fishing
camp for at least ten thousand years. So we *know* people
were in Alaska when the skulls were laid down.) That
could mean there were emerging dogs, but it would also
almost certainly mean that *C. l. pallipes* was not the sole
ancestor of our original domestic dogs. That subspecies
ranged from the area near modern Israel to the Indian
subcontinent. You don't have to spend a long time with
a map to see that Anchorage and either Tel Aviv or New
Delhi are more than a subspecies apart. Ah, the confusion
that comes from being able to live only in the present!

On the Missouri River in North Dakota, at a site called
Bagnell, there are bones that are clearly wolf and others

An attack dog of the fourteenth century.

that are just as clearly dogs. The two almost certainly were distinct enough by then so that the Indians there (that was not much more than three thousand five hundred years ago) were crossing their dogs back to the dogs' own ancestors. There could have been hybrids. They would not have been terrific in the tepee.

We hear that Eskimos routinely stake out bitches in heat so that male wolves may service them, throwing a bit of the old wolf stock back into the mix. The resultant pups/cubs would not make terrific igloodogs, but sled-pulling is the name of the game way up there and that calls for stamina and brute strength.

Neoteny, the retention of juvenile characteristics throughout life, shows up in dogs in a number of ways, including that famous the-panty-hose-don't-fit look, but neither skin wrinkles nor ear styles, none of that kind of thing, can be read in fossil evidence. All we have for certain are that skull with its apparent brain capacity, that muzzle, and those close-together teeth. If there are enough bones in one place and they are well enough associated to seem to be from the same animal, then length of leg bone, that kind of thing, can be useful. But since most of the things that might establish a dog as a dog, as opposed to a wolf, decay very quickly after the animal dies, we have these endless maybes and could-have-beens. And they are endless because although very early Canidae did evolve in North America, the family soon spread pretty much around the world.

By the middle of the Stone Age we know there were true domestic dogs widely distributed over Europe and the Middle East. In a place known as Senckenberg Bog near Frankfurt-on-Main they have unearthed a very nearly complete dog skeleton that could be eleven thousand years old near the bones of an aurochs, an extinct form of wild cattle. The aurochs' bones had been gnawed on. There were no human remains, bones or artifacts, in association. A stray middle Stone Age dog working on the carcass of a huge and surely dangerous wild bull? We will never know the story of what went on there. Would that we could.

About ten thousand years ago—when canis skulls were discovered near Fairbanks, Alaska—there were also clearly two "kinds" of dogs in what is now Denmark. There was a smaller kind (was it a subspecies, a breed of *C.f.,* or still a separate species? you decide) and a larger kind of dog as well. The big one was still a lot smaller than the local wolf strain which argues again for a more southerly origin for the dog. Those two kinds of dogs are known now as the Maglemose dogs and a carbon copy of the larger one is also known from Sweden.

There were large and small dogs from Switzerland that lived among the lake dwellers there and are known to us now as turbary dogs. From France, from Russia in an area near today's Moscow, and not long after that from the British Isles, domestic dogs coexisted with both settled and nomadic people. From Bosnia, Italy, Austria, large and small dogs are known to have been living in association with human beings. Scientists, at least many scientists, still give the big and small middle and late Stone Age dogs designations as different subspecies. Today's dogs are without those third names. With over 440 different breeds or "kinds" now recognized, subspecific names would be a nightmare, or perhaps a joke.

In the Bronze Age the medium-sized dog some scholars call *C.f. matris-optimae* may have been the ancestor of our collies, German shepherd dogs, and the other fairly long-skulled, very smart and useful breeds. That could be interesting, really important for us to know because it places potentially stock-manipulating dogs in the hands of Bronze Age man just when he began mastering flocks and herds. A great many of those dogs have been found, placing the already domesticated dog as an aid to man in the domestication of other species.

Indeed, the wolf/dog was an important bit of raw material for man to pluck from the natural world he himself evolved into. And that plucking started almost immediately. When wolves are bred in captivity reduction in size starts, amazingly enough, with the first generation. It is almost as if the dog was there waiting for man to come along and invite him in, into another kind of creature that was ready to serve, be served and share.

One of the most confounding man-and-his-dog puzzles comes from what is now Israel. At the port city of Ashkelon in southern Israel an archaeological team from the University of Alabama began digging for pottery and the like in the mid-1980s. It started out to be a typical Mideastern archaeological exercise, the kind already seen a thousand times. It is, after all, a part of the world where if you stab the earth with a stick history spurts out in a fountain of amazing finds.

They have found something far more intriguing than shards at Ashkelon, though, something quite out of the ordinary. In a relatively small area, certainly one smaller than a ball field, they have uncovered so far 785 dog graves.

They date to what is known as the Persian period, 500 to 332 B.C. Each of the relatively small dogs was buried in its own shallow pit. Pampered pets? Not likely, since only thirty-eight percent of the dogs unearthed so far had gotten beyond the puppy stage. That is the percentage for today's stray dogs, as well.

Did rabies, distemper, or some other epizootic wipe all those dogs out in a short period of time? No, the skeletons show a variety of natural causes for death. Was it just a dumping ground for dead dogs picked up in the street? Unlikely for two reasons. Each dog was in its own grave, none have been found in a common pit or hole. The limbs of the dogs were not askew, but rather neatly in place, again not dumped the way pariahs of no regard would have been. Also, none of the dogs showed signs of being disturbed once they had been buried, although their graves were quite shallow. No scavengers dug them up. That suggests that the graves were protected, watched over, cared about. None of the dogs showed signs that they had received special care while they were alive. Many had worn teeth, signs of mangled paws and broken ribs. They apparently had lived the rough life of street dogs.

At Ashkelon, in 500 B.C., Egyptian, Persian, and Phoenician cultures mixed and overlapped in ways we can barely understand. Nothing that is known about any one of those three ancient cultures would explain what has been found in that ancient port, but found it has been. Man and his dog, the more we learn the more mysterious the relationship becomes. (Do you suppose that dogs were good luck charms on boats that plied the Mediterranean—sailors always have been a superstitious lot—and when they died on board they were saved until the boat touched in at Ashkelon where they could be buried in a special cemetery? Perhaps throwing a dead dog overboard would have been considered offensive to the gods of the sea. Who can say?)

A true dog skeleton is known from Persia, found in a place called Belt Cave. It dates from between eleven and twelve thousand years ago. In Jericho (often said to be the oldest city in the world) there were fox terrier-sized dogs and pariah-style dogs (and a number of other sizes, too) perhaps nine thousand years ago, perhaps even ten. Seven thousand years ago they made figurines of what could only have been dogs in Jarmo, Iraq. At an as yet undetermined date, but a very, very long time ago, there were domestic dogs in Algeria. The saluki as we know it today is recognizable in art work from Sumeria dating back seven thousand years. At least three different breeds are known from pre-dynastic Egypt. There were greyhounds in ancient Egypt and in Spain. All over the ancient world, in fact, dogs of many kinds were carried or wandered—most likely they were first carried and then allowed to wander. And at various places at various stages of their own social development and in response to their own needs for watchdogs, guard dogs, shepherding and cattle-droving dogs, and certainly companion dogs, people bred and bred their charges again to get the characteristics that were most useful and most attractive in their eyes.

It has been suggested but not proven that there were independent centers for the domestication of the dog in the New World. A smallish subspecies of wolf from Mexico could have been the ancestor. Something like that seems almost certainly to have been the case. How else can we explain the fact that the ancient Incas mummified dogs in Peru? An eight thousand year old dog skeleton has been found in a cave in Idaho. Those dogs in Peru, it should be noted, were of several breeds, one like a modern dachshund, one like a bulldog, and one like a sheepdog. There were others, too, one of which has been likened to the greyhound. Once again to the map: just as we suspected, Peru, overlooking the Pacific Ocean, is an awful long way from Jerusalem and Jaipur.

Clearly, dogs did not cover those distances on their own. They did not climb mountains and swim oceans and navigate deserts. A dog from the proposed single center of domestication in Asia Minor would have had to do all that and more. First there would have been the Sahara Desert, either a trek across all of North Africa or a dip down south of the Atlas Mountains, followed then by a journey through the forests of central Africa, fording great rivers well populated with crocodiles until the west coast of Africa was reached.

Then there would have been the Atlantic Ocean. That would be a tough one even for an Irish water spaniel or a Portuguese water dog! Then the jungles of the Amazon or the vast savannas farther south, and then there still would have been the climb up the Andes. I think not. There are stray dogs and there are stray dogs, but that journey would take us beyond all credibility. I, for one, at least, am incredulous.

How then did they make the journey? As far as we know, there are only two ways it could have happened. Either they were carried by caravans (or tagged along— either is likely) and by boat or they made the trip genetically. The former is obvious and we know some of that did occur, a great deal of it, in fact. We are just not certain where, when, by whom, and how often. The latter means the dog was carried virtually around the world over a million or more years as a potential tucked away in the genes of the wolf *Canis lupus* in the many subspecies it would evolve into as it explored and exploited new worlds. It seems as if both of these things had to have happened, i.e., there was much more trade, exploration and cultural exchange among early peoples than perhaps we have suspected and there were multiple places where man domesticated the wolf and got the dog. Without both of those factors the geography of the dog just doesn't make sense. In fact, it appears to be impossible.

We do have to acknowledge that there have been theories about the jackal playing a role. I think it was all wolf, but at least we have acknowledged the other idea, generally discredited though it seems to be. Some Japanese inves-

Dogs of war and the hunt traveled with noble masters.

tigators over the years have proposed the smallish Japanese wolf, *C. l. hodophylax,* as a dog ancestor, stating that it somewhat resembles the dog.

The Australian dingo is another mystery entry. Most students of the subject have generally said that the dingo is a feral dog, a kind of dog carried to Australia (it certainly didn't evolve there, of that we can be sure since it is not a marsupial) by early travelers, where it escaped and became wild. Other scholars have suggested that rather than being descended from the dog we know, the dingo is ancestral to it. All of this to show just how confusing it has gotten, or perhaps always has been.

So what changes are discernible between our domesticated dog and its ancestors? We mentioned earlier that wolves lose about one-third of their brain when they become dogs and that their muzzles shorten and crowd the teeth closer together. More on the first point shortly, but what else?

In almost all domestic species except camels and horses the animals tend to get smaller. (Camels have stayed the same size, both the one- and the two-hump species, the dromedary and the bactrian, and horses have gotten considerably larger.) Dogs are smaller than wolves with the obvious exceptions of the relatively few giant breeds we have selectively bred into being—the mastiff line, the great Dane, komondor, Saint Bernard, and Newfoundland, to name a few; the giant sight hounds, borzoi, Scottish deerhound and Irish wolfhound; the greatest of the scent hounds, the bloodhound; and a few others.

Color changes are usually diagnostic of domestication. That has not been so much the case with dogs as far as range goes, pretty much because the range of colors in wild wolves is large in itself, running from frosted black to white with lemon markings. That spread has been retained in dogs with a few colors like red and blue merle added.

The placement of colors has changed, however. No one who was sober ever saw a wolf with a dalmatian's spots or the spectacular effects of harlequin Danes or the great beauty of lemon-and-white English setters. The steel-gray of the silky and Yorkshire terriers is apparently man-made. The Ibizan hound, Rhodesian ridgeback, Irish setter and chow chow all run to shades of red that are very unwolflike and the liver of the weimaraner is probably not reflected in original wild stock. Those colors and patterns are the work of selective breeding, some of which is quite recent and really very sophisticated.

In the process of domestication muzzles do tend to shorten, and not just in dogs. In horses, again in camels and in asses, this effect is not generally notable, but in most other species it does happen. In cattle, very markedly in pigs, goats, and sheep, it is easy to see. Of course, with our canine companions there have been some outlandish designer dogs created. The bulldog, pug, pekingese, Japanese chin and the English toy spaniels have all been reduced to absurd facial deformities in order to achieve fashionable styles, but even excepting the push-faces, the long-faced dogs like greyhounds, dobermans, borzois and pharaoh hounds are short in the muzzle compared with their wild and wonderful ancestors.

The above comments should not be taken as a reflection on the admirable dogginess of the push-faces. We have a pug in the crew now, our second, and have had Boston terriers and a much beloved bulldog. They can be great dogs, but they do snore with abandon and they do tend to gulp air. Gulping air can be a really taxing problem. When you have guests and you see their eyes begin to turn glassy and you see the silver candlesticks tarnish even as you look on in wonder, you know you are in for it. If your watch stops, beware. The New Zealanders have a nice expression for that phenomenon. When a previous pug we owned started to employ his weapon of mass destruction, dear Lynn Kimberling, a lady new to our shores, would chirp: *"Oh, I say. Winnie has shot a bunny."*

Our children grew up saying that and hardly anyone ever knew what they were talking about. Fortunately.

Small parts of a skeleton are not always reliable indicators of wild vs. domestic species. Unless a breed of dog has markedly deformed legs, a single leg bone may not be very helpful in distinguishing a wolf from one of its descendants. Only when man has bred doggedly (pun only partially intentional) for a strange design element—i.e., a bulldog's tail, a rottweiler's extremely wide jaws, a basset's in-part dwarf proportions—are bits and pieces of a skeleton truly indicative. Skeletal changes do generally accompany domestication, but you often need a fairly good portion of the skeleton before you know what you are dealing with, at least that is so in the case of wolves and dogs.

Hair frequently undergoes changes with domestication

and it is doubtful that that is the case with any species more than it is with dogs. Even sheep don't show the spread dogs do. Wolves have pretty much the same kind of coat all over the world where they have been found. Very northern races or subspecies have a heavier winter coat than a form from the Sinai Peninsula, but not that different. (It gets cold in the Sinai! I can testify to that.) A wolf's coat protects it from heat just as it does from cold, and just about all wolves, perhaps all, in fact, have winter and summer versions of their natural coat.

Under the loving care of man dogs now have virtually no coat (the Chinese crested dog and the Mexican hairless), weird corded coats that the dogs develop naturally at about the age of two (the puli and the komondor), thick double coats like all of the northern spitz types—the sled dogs—and hard, fine, single coats like the pointer and the greyhound. They can have hard wiry coats like most of the terriers, or soft, woolly coats like the soft-coated wheaten terrier. One breed, the dachshund, can come in three coat types: short, long and wire. The fox terriers, the chihuahua, affenpinscher and collie, also come in two, and so it goes.

Poodles have no natural maximum coat length. Their hair will grow as long as they live. They are potential hippies. The only thing that spares them that fate is our ego-inspired attentiveness. Read any book of standards. Coat types vary enormously.

When thinking about variations that have been brought about in dogs keep in mind that we generally encounter relatively few breeds in the United States. The American Kennel Club currently recognizes 135 breeds for show purposes. There are at least three hundred more breeds that the AKC has yet to acknowledge. It is not that the dogs are being kept out of the hallowed halls by some arcane exclusionary plot, but rather that there has been too little interest in them to establish studbooks and successful breeding programs here. Potentially all could be given

Chinese greyhounds, third through the tenth centuries.

AKC recognition in the future. All three hundred or so "exotic" breeds are recognized by kennel clubs in other countries, some as close by as Mexico and Canada.

Skin often undergoes changes in the process of domestication. Lots of flaps and folds are juvenile characteristics in wolves that many dogs retain throughout life. Again, our sense of aesthetics and our need for eternal babies in our pets can be seen at work. Since pet keeping undoubtedly had a great deal to do with our ever taking wolves into our lives and turning them into dogs in the first place, that is all fine and natural. Ear styles from the little prick ears of a Finnish spitz to the enormous pendular prayer rugs of the bloodhounds are things we have opted to retain or achieve.

Back to the dog's brain and the domestication process and a very important point we have saved until now. It is, in fact, a critical fact in our relationship with our pets. While it is true, as we have mentioned a couple of times, that the brain gets smaller in the journey from wolf to dog, it is only those parts that deal with sensory perception and not those centers dedicated to complex psychic processes like cognition that suffer. That is very, very important, obviously.

One of the many mysteries connected with all this is how did those early people know what they were doing? Somehow, probably with an enormous amount of trial and error, they did it. The more aesthetics developed, the more agriculture and trade gave at least certain classes of people leisure, time to think about things that were not strictly utilitarian, the more dogs became cast in beautiful and elegant forms and the larger the number of breeds that came into being. When we look at today's surviving breeds, many of them quite ancient, we are seeing not just the history of agriculture and animal husbandry, but the history of aesthetics, taste and style. When we misuse our dogs or their genes we are slashing canvases, spitting on icons, defiling precious murals with obscene graffiti. It is vandalism, pure and simple. Some of our greatest historical and artistic treasures we place with curators in museums; others we take for walks.

12

THE EAGLE was in the sky then, the serpent parted the grass, the wolf ran with the wind following the thunder of hoofs, and they all killed as they had to. And now the dogs are in my yard, holding their places not only in my heart, but in an incredible continuum, that chain of circumstances that time, chance and intelligence begot.

In passing, we have referred a number of times to the four hundred plus breeds of dogs. Are there more breeds of dogs, then, than of any other species of domestic animal? No, that prize goes to the rabbit, although the number of their breeds is really not known. And they weren't domesticated until the Middle Ages, in Spain. (The rabbits kept in ancient Rome were wild animals, trapped and kept until eaten or used in sport. The Romans didn't bother to breed even the wild ones, so they didn't bother to domesticate them.)

Still, the inventory of about 440 breeds of dogs is far too complex to lay out on a graph or for us to construct even the semblance of a family tree. It will probably never really be done. There are far too many gaps in our knowledge. Our ignorance, in fact, is profound. Since the breeds can all interbreed, except where size or some other mechanical consideration makes it just too awkward for them, poor dears, and since dogs can, do and have crossed with all manner of wolf subspecies and coyotes and perhaps even some other wild canids, too, it is all terribly mixed up and is quite probably beyond deciphering.

Before looking to the future we might take a poetic parting of the past. In his book, *Animals in Roman Life and Art,* J. M. C. Toynbee quotes the Roman poet Martial as he writes of the dog Issa, which probably was an affectionate diminutive of *Missy:*

> *Issa's more of a rogue than Lesbia's sparrow,*
> *Issa's purer by far than kiss of ring-dove,*
> *Issa's more of a coax than all the maidens,*
> *Issa's worth all the costly pearls of India,*
> *Issa's Publius' darling lady puppy.*
> *If she whimpers you'll think that she is speaking,*
> *Sorrow and joy she feels as much as he does,*
> *Snuggling close to his neck she sleeps so softly*
> *That you'd scarcely believe the pet was breathing.*

Isn't it amazing how drastically we have changed our view of our companion dogs in three thousand years! Our *moosh* factor is apparently a constant.

And where has all this brought us to, at least here in the United States? A lovely point, actually. We have a panorama of purebred dogs, at least a few to fit every imaginable taste and lifestyle. And as if that were not enough (when is enough ever enough?) the dogs themselves have taken their own libido in tow and created a seemingly infinite variety of random-bred dogs. Actually, I assume, there would be a formula that would discover that that number is finite, but I couldn't deal with it. In terms of my lack of mathematical sophistication the number is infinite. I can live with that.

Every taste *and* lifestyle? Really? I think so. At a recent reception in a magnificent home in the Pacific Heights section of San Francisco, one of the most desirable residential neighborhoods in America, I slipped canapes to a

German short-haired pointer and a thoroughly random-
bred pooch from the SFSPCA. They knew of no class
distinction. They were dogs of a feather, to use a somewhat
muddled zoological metaphor. And I have seen men and
women waiting outside of shelters, with obviously loved
and loving dogs on bits of rope.

My mother-in-law at eighty-eight has a pug that shares
her bedroom and my youngest grandchild at eighteen
months interacts splendidly with her family's dogs. In
Connecticut I have visited a teenage alcoholic in an insti-
tution who hugged his Labrador retriever while telling me
that the care of that dog was the first responsibility in his
life that he had been able to accept and deal with. I watched
through a one-way window in a geriatric home in Colum-
bus, Ohio, while a puppy was brought to a very elderly
man who had not uttered a word in months. He patted
the dog and his eyes filled with tears. There was a hidden
microphone in the room and we heard him say, very distinctly: *"I had a puppy like this when I was a boy."*

Yuppies have dogs, very often, outdoorsmen and
women certainly have them, and so do the most devout
stay-at-homes. Farmers do and suburbanites and city
dwellers all do. There is a monastery in upstate New York
where the brothers raise and train German shepherds and
I know an Episcopalian minister who has a kennel of bloodhounds. I know a rabbi who has two cocker spaniels.

At dog shows, I see more and more African-Americans
grooming and showing their dogs and lately more Americans of Asian origin. Women are, if this is possible, even
more enthusiastic about dogs than men are. (Take that as
a maybe. Let's not get sexist and crazy about this.) And
anyone who is not aware of what kids and dogs are like
has lived with their head in a paper sack.

The University of California San Francisco Medical
Center pediatric surgical unit works with the SFSPCA and
has volunteers bring dogs in to visit desperately ill children,
right into intensive care units. I met one four-year-old who

had undergone three major heart surgeries by the time he was three to correct a devastating birth defect and who suffered a massive stroke after the third. He had been seemingly in a coma and was responsive to no one and nothing until one of the volunteer's dogs was placed beside him on his bed. His mother picked up his hand and put it on the dog and little Joey moved his eyes and smiled. Everyone in the room collapsed into a sodden mass of weeping and hugging. I have interviewed both his mother and his nurse, both of whom were present. His nurse, trained so assiduously to avoid any possibility of contamination, confessed to having grave misgivings about a dog on the bed of a critically ill, apparently comatose child. Her misgivings gave way to total enthusiasm and little random-bred, obedience-trained Snickers came every day after that. In three days, Joey "walked" Snickers, taking two steps. The next day it was four steps. I witnessed Joey and Snicker's reunion a year after their first encounter. As my friend the late Herb Shriner used to say, "That can really puddle up your eyes."

I was doing a report for "20/20" at the small animal hospital of the Veterinary School of the University of Pennsylvania in Philadelphia when legendary tough guy former mayor Frank Rizzo walked in with his dog. In a conversation he referred to it as being "like one of my kids." I know a private detective and a lady cop who show dogs. Firemen have dogs at home, very often, and around the firehouse. Bill Cosby shows dogs; Jack Lemmon and his wife, Felicia, have a dog; Ben Vereen used to have a bulldog—perhaps he still does. Doris Day has lots of dogs and so do many other stars. I know for a fact that Barbara Walters and Morley Safer have had dogs (and the late Harry Reasoner) because I got their dogs for them.

Abraham Lincoln had dogs, FDR did, JFK, LBJ, RMN, and most other recent presidents did too, in the White House. George Washington had many dogs, some of them gifts from Lafayette. Daniel Webster was the first Amer-

A working Skye terrier, Flora, 1895.

ican to import Gordon setters from Scotland. Even Adolf
Hitler (as if anyone cared) had a German shepherd. It
wasn't Blondi's fault who the boss of the house was.

A vast number of portraits of old royalty show them
with dogs. Victoria loved Skye terriers, Elizabeth II is into
corgis. Mary Queen of Scots loved her toy spaniel so much
she carried it to the block with her and passed it off to a
weeping lady-in-waiting. Sir Walter Scott adored Scottish
deerhounds and George S. Patton took his bull terrier to
war with him.

That should make the point—just about every taste and
lifestyle. And how are they classified?

In America today dogs registered with the major reg-
istry, the American Kennel Club, are divided into seven
groups for purposes of showing. There is an eighth group
known, not surprisingly, as Miscellaneous where breeds
awaiting full recognition are stored. Miscellaneous breeds
are not shown in conformation competitions until after
they are moved over into one of the seven groups.

Some of the group listings are so illogical as to be bizarre and others are perfectly logical. Here is how they break down. The groups that follow are in no particular order:

THE TERRIER GROUP

There are twenty-three terriers presently recognized by the American Kennel Club. All but one of them originated in England, Scotland, Ireland, or Wales.

Airedale—the largest terrier of them all. A breed about a century old.

American Staffordshire—a bulldog-terrier cross-registered with the United Kennel Club as the American pit bull terrier.

Australian—formerly known as the Australian rough and in existence since the 1800s. Would be more logically a member of the Toy Group.

Bedlington—looks like a lamb but is actually a tough little hunting dog.

Border—one of the oldest and rarest of the terrier breeds. Developed in the English/Scottish border country.

Bull—shown in two varieties, "white" and "colored." That is a political trick to give the breed two shots instead of one in group judging. The so-called color varieties do not breed true. In one recent show I attended the colored and the white bull terriers entered were littermates. Just plain silly.

Cairn—went to Oz with Judy Garland and became very popular. A lovely doggy-looking dog.

Dandy Dinmont—the only dog named for a fictional character, a farmer in Sir Walter Scott's 1814 novel, *Guy Mannering*.

Fox—shown as one breed but in two varieties, smooth and wire. Most people's idea of the typical terrier.

Irish—an ancient terrier breed of high style and wonderful inner fire.

Kerry blue—from County Kerry in Ireland. Like many

terriers, used as a hunting and herding dog as well as a family companion.

Lakeland—from England's Lake District. A breed only about one hundred and fifty years old.

Manchester—the larger of two otherwise almost identical breeds. The other, the toy Manchester terrier, is in the Toy Group, which is perfectly logical.

Miniature schnauzer—the interloper from Germany. Very terrier-like in character, even if from across the water.

Norfolk—tiny and tough. It could be argued that this is now actually a Toy breed, although unquestionably of terrier stock.

Norwich—until recently in this country, but not in the U.K., lumped with the Norfolk terrier as one breed. Now and logically two breeds.

Scottish—one of the oldest true terrier breeds. A symbol of all the rest.

Sealyham—a Welsh breed of obscure derivation but with a devoted following.

Skye—from the Isle of Skye and the west of Scotland. At least four centuries old. A hunting breed.

Soft-coated wheaten—an Irish breed with a very soft rather than a typical wiry terrier coat. Lovely wheaten color.

Staffordshire bull—recognized in the United States only since 1975 but in England for centuries.

Welsh—sometimes confused with Irish and Lakeland terriers. If there is a typical terrier it would be this.

West highland white—a stylish Scot but not a Scottie. A breed apart with a great disposition and sense of fun.

And those are our terriers. For some reason the terriers have been declining in popularity in the United States for several decades. That is a shame because they are terrific little dogs, most of which are an ideal size for house and apartment living. They make excellent watchdogs and most are good companions for children. The Terrier Group is the most homogeneous of the seven AKC groupings.

THE NON-SPORTING GROUP

This is the AKC's catch-all group where most of the breeds are unrelated to each other in style, origin, or purpose. If I were King, I would rename it the Companion Dog Group and assign a number of other breeds to it, as I will suggest as we move along. There are currently thirteen breeds in the group, many of which are outstanding canine companions.

Bichon frise—a breed close to a thousand years old, at least. Lost to the Continent sometime after A.D. 1000 and rediscovered by Italian sailors in the Canary Islands in the 1300s.

Boston terrier—not shown as a terrier although undoubtedly a terrier-bulldog mix. One of the few truly American breeds.

Bulldog—usually referred to as English bulldog, but there is actually no English in its name. It did originate in England, however, and is a dwarf mastiff.

Chow chow—originated in China. Its name is pidgin English for bric-a-brac, which is what it was considered when purchased by English traders for export to England and the Continent. Of the northern spitz or sled-dog line.

Dalmatian—from Germany's Adriatic coast. Possibly once a hunting dog of the general continental pointer type. Very stylish.

Finnish spitz—clearly a dog of the North. These northern bushy types could have timber wolf blood added to the presumed original Middle Eastern wolf derivatives.

French bulldog—almost certainly a descendant of England's bulldog, although the French with a great deal more chauvinism than logic deny it is so. Not common in the United States.

Keeshond—another of the northern spitz-type dogs turned stylish companion. Developed in the Netherlands.

Lhasa apso—one of the Tibetan breeds held in virtually

religious regard. Probably a very ancient breed.

Standard and *miniature poodles*—the third poodle size, the toy, is shown in the Toy Group. The three are identical except for size. They may have been ancient water retrievers, but that is conjecture.

Schipperke—a breed from Belgium, known here only since the turn of the century. Very long-lived, excellent house dogs.

Tibetan spaniel—definitely not a spaniel. No one knows where these quirky names come from. It is a breed from Tibet, though, as far as we know.

Tibetan terrier—no more a terrier than the Tibetan spaniel is a spaniel. Again, though, apparently a breed from Tibet and probably quite ancient.

The catchall rather meaninglessly named Non-Sporting Group includes some of the best companion dogs on the roster. The poodles, particularly, are much beloved here and in Europe.

THE HERDING DOG GROUP

The fourteen breeds in this group are among the most intelligent and responsive of all modern breeds. They are descended from dogs that made it possible for us to reach our present high station in life. Many are still close to an original design. Their history traces the rise of man from a hunter-gatherer to pastoral and agricultural cultures.

Australian cattle dog—probably part collie and just possibly with some dingo, too. A breed still important to Australia's cattle industry.

Bearded collie—a highly intelligent breed from Scotland. Becoming quite popular in the United States.

Belgian malinois—one of three Belgian sheepherding dogs of the same general type. This breed has a short coat. These three were probably the original "police dogs."

Belgian sheepdog—the only black member of the trio. Only superficially like the German shepherd dog.

Belgian tervuren—a mahogany, well-coated member of the group. The three distinctive coats were developed and standardized early in this century.

Bouvier des Flandres—from the hill country of Belgium and France. A cattle herder and wagon puller. A powerful, useful dog on its own turf.

Briard—a French breed with a lot of service as a military pack animal. Very highly regarded by people who have owned them.

Collie—a classic breed known to all. Shown in two varieties, smooth and rough. Developed in England and Scotland.

German shepherd dog—as well known as the collie as a kind of classic dog. Very, very intelligent and performs many chores.

Old English sheepdog—despite its name, probably not more than two centuries old. Best on the farm or estate.

Puli—an old breed from Hungary, possibly originally from Tibet. It may be related to the stock that gave us the Tibetan terrier, although the coat is very different.

Shetland sheepdog—a collie in miniature from islands off Scotland where ponies and sheep have also been miniaturized. A great watchdog, to say the least. Enjoys recreational barking.

Cardigan Welsh corgi—the corgi with the tail. A tireless worker and probably from totally different stock than the Pembroke.

Pembroke Welsh corgi—the corgi without the tail. Probably the same breed known between eight and nine hundred years ago. Again, a tireless worker.

The herding dogs, until recently grouped with the working dogs, have always been popular and highly respected. They have been of great historical significance.

THE SPORTING GROUP

This large group, twenty-four breeds, contains some of the most beloved of all surviving dog breeds. Some of them are still so close to their original design that they may make less than ideal house pets. Others are among the very best house companions of all. They are a diverse and interesting group.

The pointers and setters mark the game for the hunter, the spaniels (from *Spanish* dogs) flush game from cover, and the retrievers bring it back to the hunter after it has been shot. That was the original plan.

A good many dogs that are used in hunting—terriers and hounds, for example—are not listed as sporting dogs. That is because this group takes origin into account. Spaniels and setters are from a common origin—the setters worked on land, and some spaniels may have worked in water. The group as a whole was derived on the Continent and the British Isles. There has been American influence, as well.

Brittany—not "Brittany spaniel," as it used to be. A hard-working setterlike dog from France. No doubt had common origin with setters and spaniels long ago.

Pointer—a typical Continental hard-coated field dog, literally points to game. May be one of the oldest of the true hunting breeds. Well known in England by the mid-1600s but certainly older than that across the Channel.

German short-haired pointer—a German-Austrian development of the last century. Probably the descendant of an old Spanish pointer now extinct. Has webbed feet and retrieves as well as points.

German wire-haired pointer—another recent development, probably dating no further back than the 1870s or 1880s. A rugged hunter with a water-repellent coat.

Chesapeake Bay retriever—a true American breed whose history began in 1807. Tradition has a British ship sinking

off Maryland. Landsmen went to the rescue and among
the survivors were some hunting dogs that were crossed
with a rough local retriever. The Chessie was the result,
so the story goes.

Curly-coated retriever—a nineteenth century British development seen in America for the first time in 1907. May
have some poodle genes and some from an extinct breed
known as Saint John's dog.

Flat-coated retriever—developed in England, using both
European and North American breeds. No more than a
century or so old. Not well known in America but highly
regarded.

Golden retriever—developed within the last century from
the flat-coated retriever and the now extinct tweed spaniel.
A single breeding produced four puppies and down from
them has come one of the most beloved of all dog breeds.
Money grubbers have done their best to ruin the breed by
mass production, but there are still wonderful goldens to
be had from knowledgeable, caring breeders.

Labrador retriever—not a product of Labrador at all, but
Newfoundland. Actually developed in England from 1820
on. If there are five greatest dog breeds of all places and
all times, the "Lab" is among them. A superlative breed
of dog in the field, on the farm, in the home.

English setter—a breed dating back at least four centuries.
Probably down from a Spanish pointer and several different spaniels. A great beauty; a work of art.

Gordon setter—what England can do, the Scots can do.
A development by the Duke of Gordon. As indicated earlier, first specimens here were imported by Daniel Webster. A particularly sweet-tempered dog.

Irish setter—and what the English and the Scots can do,
by golly, the Irish can do. This is the Irish entry into one
of dogdom's ultimate beauty contests, dating from the last
century. Originally red and white.

American water spaniel—a true native American from the
Midwest. Probably down from the larger Irish water span-

iel and the curly-coated retriever. A rare breed, little known but well-liked by those who do know it.

Clumber spaniel—the bulkiest of the spaniels; not common but registered by the AKC as far back as 1883. Quite unlike the other spaniels in style, but a true hunting companion.

Cocker spaniel—the American version of an English development from a Spanish dog. Again a political bit of one-upmanship. Shown in three color varieties in the group: black, parti-color, and ASCOB. The latter means "any solid color other than black." Historically, as a true spaniel, logically belongs here. But if there were a Companion Dog Group, as I would create to absorb the Non-Sporting Group, the cockers would go there. No longer a field dog.

English cocker spaniel—dates from at least the 1300s and may be older than that. The source for the American version which has become a very different dog. It wasn't until 1946 that the split was established.

English springer spaniel—springs game. A root stock breed giving rise to many of the other spaniels we know today. Shown in America since 1910.

Field spaniel—a kind of cocker spaniel in the last century but long since a breed apart. Not well known at all but reputedly a very nice animal.

Irish water spaniel—tallest of all the spaniels. Imported from Ireland before the Civil War. Looks a bit like a clown but performs like a true field dog. A serious dog.

Sussex spaniel—another rare breed in this country. A heavily built spaniel for rough terrain. From the English county of Sussex.

Welsh springer spaniel—described at least as far back as 1570 but probably known in Wales and the west of England before that. Not common in America. Has also been known as the "starter" or "starter spaniel."

Vizsla—Hungary's most famous hunting dog. An all-purpose continental hunting dog, probably down from some hound and a Transylvanian pointer. Becoming better known here every year.

Weimaraner—developed in Germany in the 1900s. A closely guarded treasure. You had to belong to a club to even buy one. Highly regarded for all kinds of field work.

Wire-haired pointing griffon—a dog of the Netherlands, later popular with both German and French hunters. A connoisseur's dog, not terribly well known in this country.

And that is the roster of the gun dogs. It is a pity, in a way, that such really beautiful breeds had to have hunting as an excuse for being. No doubt, though, hunters have been among the most careful and imaginative of breed designers and that is what these breeds are, designed to perform special roles for extremely demanding owners.

THE HOUND GROUP

Twenty-one breeds of dogs are shown as hounds by American Kennel Club rules. Some are perfectly logical, some totally illogical in this group. We shall come to them. Basically, the logical hounds are divided into two categories, the gaze or sight hounds and the scent hounds, those that hunt with their eyes and those that are guided almost exclusively by their noses.

Some of the most interesting and historically significant of all known breeds still with us are included in the hound group, and not just a few that are enigmatic.

Afghan—a breed known since at least 4000 B.C. Apparently carried across Arabia and Persia, perhaps as trade goods, and eventually established in northern Afghanistan. Regally handsome, powerful, and swift, a venerable dog of great historical interest. A true sight hound.

Basenji—from somewhere in Africa, found in both Egypt and the Congo. The history of the breed is a total mystery and its inclusion with the hounds is without basis.

Mr. Everette Millais's basset hound, Model, 1895.

Should be in the not-yet-established Companion Dog Group.

Basset—from Belgium and France, a true scenting *hawnddawg*. Incredible disposition and sense of humor. Only for people who deserve them.

Beagle—a true scent hound. Shown in two varieties, up to 13 inches tall and up to 15 inches at withers. Fine as pets individually, but often maintained in packs.

Black-and-tan coonhound—of a number of coonhounds known in the American South, this is the only one recognized by the AKC. Descendant of the bloodhound. An active coon-hunting dog and a good pet.

Bloodhound—a true giant, up to 150 pounds. Ancient, to 2500 B.C., at least, in Rome. Foundation breed for most if not all of today's scent hounds. Very gentle and affectionate.

Borzoi—known as Russian wolfhound until 1936. Regal, does vodka commercials. A giant sight hound descended from greyhound stock.

Dachshund—the German badger hound. Used to be much larger than today's dog. Comes in two sizes, standard and miniature, but sizes are not distinguished in the ring. It is shown in three coat styles, however—longhaired, smooth, and wire-haired—so there are really six dachshunds!

American foxhound—first imported into the United States as English foxhounds in 1742. More were brought in in 1770 by George Washington and still more in 1785 by Lafayette as gifts for Washington. Usually maintained in packs.

English foxhound—the original. Relatively rare in this country, especially as house pets. A pack hound, usually, with a great deal of tradition.

Greyhound—at least since the time of Christ, mostly in Egypt. One of the true foundation breeds from which many of today's sight hounds are descended. Lovely, gentle dogs steeped in rich tradition.

Harrier—not an ancient breed as some stories state. Undoubtedly a recent offshoot of the foxhound line. Very much like the foxhounds in all ways.

Ibizan hound—at least to 3600 B.C. in Egypt. Exceptionally elegant sight hound of the greyhound type. Virtually identical to statues of dogs that guarded the tombs of the pharaohs. Much beloved by owners. Still relatively rare. A chance to own living history.

Irish wolfhound—a true giant, tallest of all modern dog breeds. Was nearly extinct by 1860, but rebuilt from what little stock was left by a British army officer. A splendid but unfortunately short-lived dog. Seldom lives to be even nine years old. Gigantism in dogs is a fatal "disease."

Norwegian elkhound—a companion of the Vikings dating back thousands of years. A true northern spitz type. No more a hound than it is a chihuahua. Totally illogical in the hound group.

Otter—sometimes referred to as a bloodhound with a coat. Used in packs to hunt otters and protect salmon and trout streams in England in the nineteenth century, but probably much older than that.

Pharaoh—one of the oldest of all modern breeds, goes back at least seven thousand years. Probably taken to Malta by Phoenicians where it was preserved. Great historical breed, still of high style and merit.

Rhodesian ridgeback—developed by European settlers in the southern third of Africa nearly three centuries ago. Actually used to hunt lions. Assignment to the Hound Group seems less logical than to the Sporting Group.

Saluki—traces back to Sumeria at least seven thousand years. Called the "royal dog of Egypt." One of the most elegant of the sight hounds. Pretty much the same now as it was in ancient times.

Scottish deerhound—another true giant descendant of greyhounds. Sir Walter Scott called them "the most perfect creatures of heaven." Deeply loved and admired by their fanciers.

Whippet—undoubtedly a miniaturized descendant of greyhound stock. Fast and extremely elegant, wonderful house pets.

Lumped together in the Hound Group are some of the truly great chapters in the history of the domestic dog. When we say a breed goes back at least three or four thousand years we are referring to the known representations of that breed on pottery, murals, textiles and other works of art. Surely some of the breeds go back much, much further than that. The hounds are history, art history, technological history, the history of husbandry, the history of cultures, and both vanishing and evolving civilizations. They are among our most precious ancient artifacts, yet they live to love and amuse us. In a way it is a miracle.

THE TOY GROUP

These are the knickknacks of the dog world. Some, like the Italian greyhound, the Pomeranian and the toy Manchester terrier, have been reduced in size to be toy companions while others evolved that way from earlier toy stock. These are really working dogs, but their work is to please, amuse, help their owners battle loneliness. Their task is to be needed and they virtually always are needed wherever they are found. Anyone who puts these dogs down because of their high froufrou quotient is suffering from absurd macho-itis. These are the biggest dogs in the world in small carry-on packages. There are seventeen breeds in the group.

Affenpinscher—was known in Europe at least as far back as the seventeenth century. A foundation breed from which many other Toy breeds were built. Should be classed as a monkey. A born entertainer.

Brussels griffon—down in part from the affenpinscher, a dog of Belgium. Seen in both rough and smooth coats, but not so distinguished in show ring. Great clowns.

Chihuahua—has a strange history, but apparently was brought to Mexico from China a very long time ago. It is difficult to imagine by whom. Shown in two coat varieties, long and smooth. Generally thought of as the smallest of all breeds still known today. May be the smallest ever.

English toy spaniel—popular with British royal family since Elizabeth I's time. Shown in two varieties, dictated by color only; there is the *Blenheim and Prince Charles* and the *King Charles and Ruby*. Stylish and elegant, but not yet too popular in this country. Probably is in part shrunken spaniel stock.

Italian greyhound—has been around for at least two millennia. Is a vest-pocket version of greyhound brought down in size to be a lap-sitter, which standard greyhounds most assuredly are not.

Japanese chin—one of the oldest of all Toy breeds. Very aristocratic. Small but carries a lot of class, history, and tradition.

Maltese—at least twenty-eight centuries old and perhaps even older than that. Favored by royalty for centuries. Refined and elegant little creatures of style and personality.

Toy Manchester terrier—a shrunken version of the standard designed for the lap and the cushion. Retains terrier spirit and would love to kill rats, if you'd let him, at least very small ones.

Miniature pinscher—this is not, repeat not, a shrunken Doberman as many people seem to believe. As a breed it is very much older than the dobie and just because they both look like lugers does not mean they are connected. They are not.

Papillon—dates back to Spain, France and Italy at least to the sixteenth century and probably earlier than that. Its enormous widespread ears do make it look like a *papillon* or butterfly.

Pekingese—the symbolic toy. From China at least as far back as the eighth century. Seen by the Western world in 1860 when the British looted the Imperial Palace. The Chinese killed most of them to keep their precious secret dog from being seen by Western world. That would seem to be something of an overreaction.

Pomeranian—a true Arctic spitz type that weighed from twenty to thirty-five pounds when first brought here from Germany. Reduced to pocket size and now a true Toy.

Toy poodle—one of the most popular Toys or dogs, for that matter, of modern times. Definitely a shrunken dog of great style and intelligence. A flawless house or apartment companion. Best seen on fluffy cushions eating bonbons.

Pug—a Chinese dog, not Dutch, although very popular in the Netherlands. Largest of all Toys, larger in fact than the Boston terrier which is shown in the Non-Sporting Group. Clearly illogical.

Shih tzu—a special Toy of the Chinese emperor. Becoming very popular in the United States whence it came from China after a long layover in England.

Silky terrier—an Australian contribution clearly related to the Australian terrier and another Toy, the Yorkshire terrier.

Yorkshire terrier—one of the most enduringly popular of all Toys. First seen in England at a dog show in Leeds in 1870s when it weighed up to fifteen pounds. Now you can practically weigh one on a postage scale.

The Toys are stunning little dogs that exhibit one of the domestic dog's most endearing charms: they never grow up. They remain tiny children for as long as they live and that gives purpose to the lives of the people who own them. To laugh at a Toy is to laugh at human emotional needs. These are among the most skilled therapists in dog-dom. They are little gems.

THE WORKING DOG GROUP

Until 1982 the dogs in this group were combined under this heading with the dogs presently listed as Herding Dogs. The group got out of hand, however—thirty-three breeds. This breakout of nineteen Working Dogs and four-teen Herding Dogs makes more sense although there are, as usual, some strange inconsistencies.

The Working Dogs can be viewed as two subgroups. There are the guard dogs and watchdogs and the sled dogs of that old northern spitz type. Therein lies one grave inconsistency. The three Belgian sheepdog breeds and the German shepherd, among the best guard dogs of all, ended up with the Herding Dogs although few have been used that way for years. Still, you have to put them someplace and there can be only one group to a customer.

Akita—from Akita Province, Island of Honshu, Japan, and known here only since the end of World War II. A large, powerful guard dog. Becoming very popular.

Alaskan malamute—a dog of the North, a typical sled

dog/northern spitz type. *Note:* Why aren't the keeshond and the Norwegian elkhound in this group?

Bernese mountain dog—a Swiss dog, undoubtedly down from the mastiff line. From the canton of Berne. Handsome, robust dogs.

Boxer—another mastiff derivative. Among the most handsome of all dogs, but not as popular as they once were. A German design.

Bullmastiff—an English idea, a cross between the mastiff and the bulldog to help gamekeepers patrol their bosses' estates. Dates to the late 1800s.

Doberman pinscher—from Germany, and the 1890s. Down from rottweilers and sheepdogs. Designed to be the ultimate guard and police dog by Ludwig Dobermann.

Giant schnauzer—again Germany and again the last part of the last century. A cart puller, a herder, a guard dog. An all-purpose dog of great stamina.

Great Dane—Germany, not Denmark, a mastiff derivative designed to hunt dangerous wild boar. A giant and a gentleman of high style.

Great Pyrenees—an ancient breed whose purpose is to guard sheep, not herd them. The story is that General Lafayette brought the first ones to the United States in 1824.

Komondor—from Hungary, a guardian of the flocks, not a herder. Absolutely fearless. Can tolerate any weather.

Kuvasz—another Hungarian herd guard, at least a thousand years old. The dog's origin is a mystery that we may never be able to solve.

Mastiff—one of the most important breeds still with us. A true foundation animal that gave rise to many, many breeds and contributed genes to a great many others. Probably started in Tibet (but how?) and was taken to Rome, then up through Europe. Mystery: when the Roman legions with their mastiff war dogs reached the British Isles, the "savages" there already had their own mastiff. How?

Newfoundland—probably did originate in Newfoundland a couple of hundred years ago and may have had Great Pyrenees genes. A massive dog of willing spirit and natural good manners.

Portuguese water dog—known for centuries in the Algarve. May have come there from the Middle East. May have some common ancestry with the poodles. May be the ancestor of the Irish water spaniel. A lot of "maybes" with this old breed.

Rottweiler—a German designer dog from the Roman legions' mastiff line. A very rough, tough dog, best owned by assertive people. Not an ideal pet for wimps.

Saint Bernard—a Swiss derivation from the mastiff line. The keg of brandy was once added by a painter as a dramatic touch. There is fact and fiction in the history of this breed. Trouble is, you can't always tell which is which.

Samoyed—a very ancient dog from Siberia, a dog of the Samoyed people. Typical northern spitz design. Sled puller and guard, this is an all-purpose animal and stunningly beautiful, too.

Siberian husky—another dog of the North and obviously a sled dog. Much beloved by experienced owners.

Standard schnauzer—a stable dog from at least the Middle Ages and perhaps earlier than that. A breed apart from both the giant and the miniature schnauzers. Powerful ratters and attentive watchdogs.

And with that we end our list of present-day AKC breeds. The list will continue to grow as people become more and more enchanted by breeds they encounter in their travels abroad. We still have more than three hundred to choose from. Without doubt some of the breeds listed will become extinct as fewer people show interest in them. Domestic animals of many kinds, not just dogs, are endangered, just as species of wildlife are. It takes enthusiasm, time, space, and money to keep species or breeds alive. And we humans are a fickle lot. As bemoaned earlier, it would be wonderful to be able to spend a few hours in the past. The same could be said of the future.

The genetic manipulation that was done to give us our dogs has been, as suggested earlier, costly. Our dogs have undeniable genetic faults that we will eventually eliminate. Examples:

The affenpinscher is listed as being subject to seven hereditary diseases, or genetic faults, including cleft palate and bad knees. The latter can be crippling.

The Afghan hound is down for five, things ranging from unwarranted sensitivity to flea collars, to cataracts, corneal dystrophy and elbow joint malformation.

Airedales are apparently rather sturdy stock with only three inherited health problems recorded. Japan's akita is down for three, but no mention is made of the terrible orthopedic problems that the current breeding practices in America have caused. Dropping the hind legs straight down on such a large dog is an impossible design.

The Alaskan malamute is a seven-faulter while the basenji has eight genetic quirks that can mean veterinary bills, not to mention pain and discomfort for the animals. The Australian shepherd has ten potential defects while the Australian cattle dog is not known to have any. That is a strange twist. Both breeds were bred for utility far more than for conformation. The basset hound (whenever I look at our Lizzie I have to wonder what the designers were trying to do) has no less than thirteen potential genetic faults.

The beagle, with everything from epilepsy to glaucoma to missing kidneys, is shown to have twenty-three potential health problems that can be traced to genetics. The Boston terrier has twenty-seven on its list. The boxer is down for twenty-three, the bulldog for thirty-nine! Well, that is an absurd design, even if the dog is a love. The cocker spaniel, American version, has forty, which is prob-

ably the record, and the collie has twenty. The rough and
tough German shepherd dog has a potential for twenty-
five hereditary faults or problems. None are known for
the harrier, but again twenty-five for, of all things, the
beloved Labrador retriever. The Norwich terrier has a
clean genetic bill of health, the poodles have no less than
twenty-six bad health characteristics on the chart, the Saint
Bernard twenty, some of them lethal when and if they
occur, and so it goes. If you want the whole list and a
medical-potential profile of each breed, the reference is
Medical and Genetic Aspects of Purebred Dogs, edited by Ross
D. Clark, D.V.M. and Joan R. Stainer, 1983, Veterinary
Medicine Publishing Company, Edwardsville, Kansas.

The genetic fault-potential chart hardly suggests that the
breeds listed are going to have all of these problems. Far
from it. Most of the dogs you know will go through life
with no such case histories. The chart, which like all things
constructed by man is almost certainly incomplete and
imperfect, does say that breeding for style, beauty and even
utility has its problems. It is going to take much more
breeding by very genetics-savvy people in consultation
with their veterinarians to keep the species *Canis familiaris*
from falling even further into a trap. We may be close to
stretching the wolf's potential for the dog a little too thin
and it may be time to back off. There can't be too many
new uses for the dog so that we need to carve out that
many more new breeds. Perhaps it is time to perfect what
we have and show a little genetic mercy. If we feel we
need more breeds in the United States, there are over three
hundred others worldwide, a whole supermarket full of
dog breeds where we can go shopping. Many of those
breeds are quite old, in the hundreds of years, and some
very, very old, in the thousands of years. In any case we
should concentrate on getting out the bad traits and paying
due respect to the history of those canine genes.

As for mixed-breed dogs (my name for them is the rather
more dignified "random-bred"), Lord love 'em, we always

have some. They are as fulfillingly doggy as any pure breed
and deserving of just as much care. It is just plain nonsense
to suppose they need less because they don't come with a
fancy kennel name attached. We must stop encouraging
or allowing random-bred animals (dogs or cats) from
breeding, however, since we are killing well over twelve
million a year because there are not enough homes. For
the time being that means surgery although a chemical
solution to the problem will soon be available. No dog,
pure-bred or random-bred, should ever become a parent
unless it is an excellent example of its breed and its genes
are really needed to perpetuate a historically valid line.

There is a lightly supported and I think very unwise idea
(I don't believe it is anything as important as a movement)
that purebred dogs shouldn't be allowed to reproduce
either. Think of what that means. Within ten years, twelve
at the very most, given their life spans, all of the giant dog
breeds would be extinct. In just that decade we would lose

*Lurcher: a crossbred dog, properly between the collie and the greyhound,
largely used by poachers.*

all of the mastiff line, the Newfoundland, Bernese mountain dog, Great Dane and Saint Bernard, the Irish
wolfhound, Scottish deerhound, bloodhound, komondor,
Great Pyrenees, kuvasz, and a number of others, some of
which have been with us for between one and three thousand years. In that same decade, plus a year or two, all of
the medium to large dogs would probably have gone past
the point of no return in their sexual potential and their
breeds would also be functionally extinct. Give it another
six or eight years and between ten and twenty thousand
years of man's intense love affair with the child of the wolf
would be over. I assume the people who do not want any
more greyhounds or golden or Labrador retrievers to be
born would also mandate that random-bred dogs also be
exterminated. What a dastardly scheme! There is terrible
human overpopulation, too, and high mortality from war
and disease. Is genocide the answer?

Surely, as rational and potentially compassionate human
beings we must find ways to deliver veterinary care where
it is needed to stop the overproduction of companion animals. It is a mortal sin the way it is now, but the dog
must survive for its utility, its absolute beauty, its love of
us and our love of it. The loss of the dogs in our lives is
unthinkable and any suggestion that it be a goal is quite
thoroughly mad.

Unfortunately, dogs have been the subject of fads, and
fads are frequently tied in with some machismo nonsense.
One that has been growing in the United States and Canada
is crossing dogs back to wolves or wolf hybrids and then
trying to make house pets out of the resulting mixed species
animals. Wolf/dog crosses cannot be housebroken, they
certainly can't be punished, they should be double-fenced
and/or chained because if they get loose there can be all
hell to pay. They are, by the way, useless as watchdogs
and not in the least protective. They are rarely safe around
children and a good many deaths and mutilations have
occurred in the last couple of decades.

There are reports of perfectly nice wolf/dog hybrids that are easily housebroken, wonderful with children and other animals and "are just like any good housedog." They are easy to explain. They are housedogs. Whenever there is a buck to be made someone will be out there with a crooked scheme. Many unscrupulous breeders have been crossing German shepherd dogs with Alaskan malamutes and Siberian huskies and selling the somewhat wolfish looking puppies as dog/wolf crosses. They haven't had wolf in them, in most cases, for fifteen thousand years. Sure, they act like housedogs, they are mixed breeds but full-blooded *Canis familiaris*.

Since our dogs came from wolves and brought so many wonderful traits with them, why is it such a disaster to cross dogs back to wolves to create interesting pets? First, the wolf's admirable traits are admirable for the wolf, but not for the dog. Those traits were convertible and we converted them to make the dog idea work. One good trait for wolves but bad for dogs we had to get rid of is that wolves are afraid of people. Wolves and primitive man and before them prehominids were together long enough in the same habitats for the wolf to work that fear into its survival package. That is why there are no records over the last few centuries at least of healthy wolves attacking human beings. The throw-the-baby-from-the-troika legend is just that, a legend. Even the Russians admit that. Rabid wolves have attacked people, but rabid anythings will attack anything.

But we made dogs not to fear us and when you breed that not-to-fear characteristic back into a part-wolf, therein lies potential trouble. In short, a wolf/dog cross is a messed-up mixture of genes, traits and characteristics that doesn't belong to either world, the wild one out there or the one in our backyard or, heaven forbid, in our living room. Crossing dogs back to wolves for a lark is a perfectly terrible idea. The animal is likely to end up badly, unadoptable, and killed early in its life. Unfortunately a child may get killed along the way. Genes are not for mucking about with, not unless someone really knows what they are doing and has an excellent reason for doing it.

The future and the fate of the dog, of all animals, of course, are in our hands. Every animal on the earth deserves our consideration and the most intelligent application of what we have come to know of life and living systems that we can offer. As far as I know, there is no set point when evolution stops, when a species is all done with the ride on the point of its spear as it penetrates the fabric of time. I will admit that there hasn't seemed to have been a heck of a lot of action in the horseshoe crab line lately and the scorpions and cockroaches seem to be pretty much settled into a lifestyle that suits them in the environments they inhabit. Still, we can't say they have reached the end of their lines.

I think we can say for certain, though, that the dog is not there. The wolf from which it arose is not all that old a species, the extracted dog is only moments old in the history of life, and we have done a lot of fooling around in the process of extracting a species to suit our needs and tastes. There is this, too. We are evolving, without a doubt that is true. No one can possibly say what we will be like in five hundred or a thousand years. With the move toward space, and that is absolutely inevitable whatever other priorities we may seem to have at the moment, the move into the sea for exploration and later exploitation, with the progress of medicine, who knows what we will become not only at the hands of evolution but by our own hands as well. When cancer, diabetes, geriatric deterioration, stroke, obesity, and heart attacks are ancient history, what will we then live long enough to get or become?

Since we have such a profound effect on our companion animals, what effect will our changing selves have on them? Advances in the still very young science of veterinary medicine are already stunning and things will continue to move forward on that front. Our own world and therefore what we can offer our animals will change and, somewhat more slowly, the dog's species will continue to evolve. It may take rather a long time for the dog to sort out the things we have done to it already before it can get back down to just good old-fashioned evolution on its own, of course.

At any rate, the evolution of the dog as a discrete species has barely begun. As domesticators we have plugged ourselves into the creation process. That has never happened before in the history of life on this planet. One species, lo these last ten to twenty thousand years, has willingly and knowingly, more willingly and knowingly lately than at the beginning of the process, made itself part of the design and destiny of other species. And at the head of the class of our subjects is the dog. We are rather like co-founders, in cooperation with nature, of course, but very active participants in building the species from the ground up. No one will ever be able to say with any certainty exactly where or when the wolf spun off into the dog, when the newer species can be said to have actually come into being, but whenever and wherever it was, there we were pushing buttons and spinning dials.

If you have a dog (and I consider that quite likely) and you have read any of these paragraphs aloud, your dog has been listening to you. Perhaps all of the words weren't clear to your friend, but your tone and attitude were. If your attitudes or beliefs about your dog have changed, however unconsciously or imperceptibly because of something you have read, your dog has picked up on that change. Our dogs are tuned into us like radar dishes and we, like interstellar space, are constantly being probed.

However much we would like to understand our dogs, that is how badly our dogs would like to understand us. We are players on a team, and we should always be aware of that. Our dogs are endlessly willing to join in a mutually pleasing arrangement. He or she will do his or her part to be faithful, loyal, loving, to listen and pay attention. I hope as much can be said for us.

PICTURE SOURCES

Metropolitan Museum of Art
    pages 14, 65, 77, 87, 125
New York Public Library Picture Collection
    pages 16, 29, 39, 43, 49, 57, 60, 62, 67, 90, 93, 96, 99, 121,
    127, 134, 139, 149, 155, 161, 166, 172, 179, 187, 193, 197,
    223, 228
Sarah Fowler
    page 20
Jill Freedman
    pages 23, 36, 46, 59, 85, 103, 107, 116, 158
Karen Sanborn
    pages 33, 74, 144, 169
Library of the General Society of Mechanics and Tradesmen
    pages 52–53, 78, 82, 113, 129, 183, 203, 213
Yale Center for British Art, Paul Mellon Collection
    page 73
Drawings by Hilary Knight from *Eloise* by Kay Thompson
    page 84
T. Charles Erickson
    page 131

INDEX

ABOUT THE AUTHOR

ROGER CARAS has written over fifty-five books on pets and wild-life, as well as magazine articles for *The New York Times Magazine, Ladies Home Journal, The National Observer,* and scores of other magazines and journals. Mr. Caras has made hundreds of guest appearances on radio and television throughout the United States and Canada and was affiliated with the ABC Television Network for seventeen years as the first and only special correspondent for animals and the environment. He is now president of the American Society for the Prevention of Cruelty to Animals.